THE THAMES

CLXX

CLXX

1 Eton College and Chapel from the River

From a drawing by W. Westall, A.R.A., engraved by R. G. Reeves, circa 1828

THE THAMES

FROM MOUTH TO SOURCE

By

L. T. C. Rolt

*Illustrated in Colour from
Old Water Colours
and Aquatints*

*With Notes on the Artists and
Illustrations by*

Francis Maxwell

CLXX

B. T. BATSFORD LTD

LONDON   NEW YORK
TORONTO   SYDNEY

First Published, 1951

Printed and bound in Great Britain by William Clowes and Sons Ltd
London and Beccles for the Publishers
B. T. BATSFORD LTD. LONDON: 15 North Audley Street, W.1 & Malvern Wells
Worcestershire. NEW YORK: 122 East 55th Street
TORONTO: 103 St. Clair Avenue West. SYDNEY: 156 Castlereagh Street

PREFACE

THE books on the Thames published during the last century and a half would fill a good-sized library, yet, undeterred by their crowd of predecessors, modern authors are continually adding to them with contributions often distinctly worth while. Many artists have depicted their impressions of the river in a variety of styles and media, and it is fortunate that several series of aquatints by such artists as Robert Havell, William Westall, A.R.A., John Boydell, Joseph Farington, R.A. and Samuel Owen have been devoted to the course of the Thames. With a selection of the work of these artists it was decided to include some reproductions specially made from the extensive but little-known and unpublished series of water-colours by George Shepherd in the Sutherland Collection, long a valued feature of the Bodleian Library but recently transferred to the Ashmolean Museum, Oxford. These form part of the extraordinary series of Grangerized large folio volumes, over fifty in all, of Clarendon's *History of the Rebellion* and Burnet's *History of Our Own Times*, which represent perhaps the most extensive and elaborate achievement in extra-illustration extant. George Shepherd was apparently commissioned to make a series of watercolours of places and scenes connected with the Civil War, and this included a number of Thames-side subjects, particularly those at strategically important river crossings. Two plates of towns on typical tributaries: Witney, on the Wind-rush, and Tonbridge, on the Medway, together with several other characteristic watercolours, have been included. In all, the work of fourteen artists is represented.

Mr. L. T. C. Rolt, whose wide knowledge and love of England's inland waterways is well known, and has been recorded in his writings, has placed these old illus-trations in a present-day setting by contributing an account of the River from its seamouth to its source, and this has been supplemented by notes on the artists represented and brief descriptions of the plates.

Summer 1951   THE PUBLISHERS

v

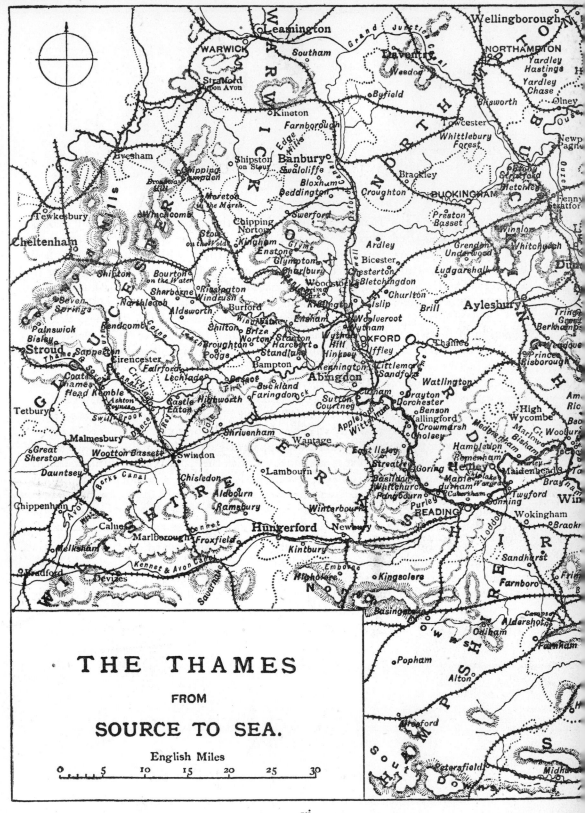

THE THAMES

FROM

SOURCE TO SEA.

English Miles

0   5   10   15   20   25   30

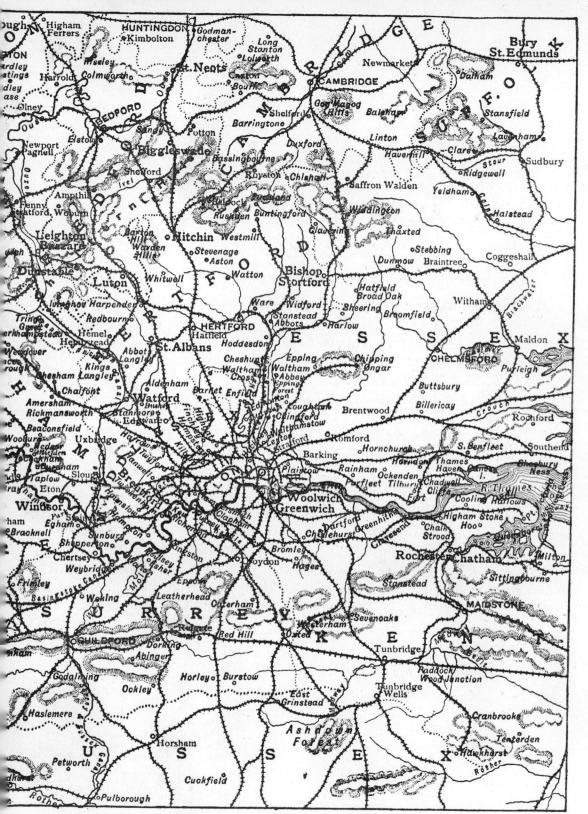

ACKNOWLEDGMENT

Figure 12 is reproduced by gracious permission of His Majesty the King.

The Publishers are indebted to the following for permission to reproduce originals as shown:

Messrs. M. Knoedler & Co. Ltd., for facilities for including figs. 6 and 13, which are now in the collection of William Hartmann Esq.

Messrs. Frank T. Sabin, for fig. 5.

The Trustees of the Ashmolean Museum, Oxford, for figs. 16, 22, 24, 27 and 28.

The Council for the Preservation of Rural England, for fig. 26.

The Trustees of the Victoria and Albert Museum, for figs. 14 and 15.

Miss Norah Davenport, for the line drawing on page 75.

Miss Irene Hawkins, for the line drawing on page 30, from a photograph by E. W. Tattersall, Esq.

Messrs. Longmans Green & Co. Ltd., for the line drawing by E. H. New from the *Life of William Morris* by J. W. Mackail, reproduced on page 56.

Thanks are also due to Mrs. Owen and Messrs. Chatto & Windus for their kind permission to quote the poem 'Shadwell Stair' by the late Wilfred Owen.

CONTENTS

BIBLIOGRAPHY

A FEW SELECTED REPRESENTATIVE BOOKS ON THE THAMES

W. BOYDELL and J. FARINGTON, R.A., *History of the River Thames*, 2 vols., 4to., 1794–96.

R. HAVELL, *A Series of Picturesque Views of the River Thames*, Fol., 1811.

W. WESTALL and S. OWEN, *Picturesque Tour of the River Thames,* Fol., 1828.

TOMBLESON's *The Thames.* 80 engraved views. Text by W. G. Fearnside. Small 4to, *ca.* 1830.

S. C. HALL, *The Book of the Thames.* 4to. 1859.

JOHN TAYLOR, the Water Poet, *Thame Isis* (in *Works*, 1st collection 1870.)

VARIOUS AUTHORS, *Rivers of Great Britain: The Thames.* (vol. one.) 4to, *ca.* 1892 (2 vols., *ca.* 1885–95).

DEAN CHURCH, *Isis and Tamesis*, 8vo, 1886.

J. ASHBY-STERRY, *The Lay of the Lazy Minstrel*, Small 8vo, 1886.

W. ARMSTRONG, *The Thames from its Rise to the Nore*, 4to, *ca.* 1890.

JEROME K. JEROME, *Three Men in a Boat*, 8vo, *ca.* 1890.

T. R. WAY, *Reliques of Old London upon the Banks of the Thames*, 4to, 1899.

ELIZABETH R. and J. PENNELL, *The Stream of Pleasure*, 8vo, *ca.* 1900.

MATTHEW ARNOLD, *The Scholar Gipsy*, and *Thyrsis*, 8vo, 1906.

HILAIRE BELLOC, *Historic Thames*, 8vo, 1909.

HILAIRE BELLOC, *River of London*, 8vo, 1912.

F. S. THACKER, *Thames Highway*, 1914.

H. M. TOMLINSON, *London River*, 8vo, 1921.

A. WILLIAMS, *Round about the Upper Thames*, 8vo, 1922.

H. M. TOMLINSON, *Gallions Reach*, 8vo, 1927.

W. R. DAVIDGE, *South Buckinghamshire and Thames-side Report*, 1928.

A. G. LINNEY, *Peepshow of the Port of London*, 8vo, 1929.

COUNCIL FOR THE PRESERVATION OF RURAL ENGLAND, *Report on the Thames Valley from Cricklade to Staines*, 1929.

DONALD MAXWELL, *A Pilgrimage of the Thames*, 8vo, 1932.

R. GIBBINGS, *Sweet Thames Run Softly*, 8vo, 1940.

S. R. JONES, *Thames Triumphant*, Large 8vo, 1943.

LONDON COUNTY COUNCIL, *The County of London Plan*, 4to, 1944.

J. H. O. BUNGE, *A Tideless Thames in a Future London*, 1944.

M. SHAW BRIGGS, *Down the Thames*, 8vo, 1946.

JOHN RODGERS, *English Rivers*, 8vo, 1947.

MIDDLESEX AND SURREY C.C.C. JOINT COMMITTEE, *Report on the Thames from Putney to Staines*, 1948.

J. HERBERT, *The Port of London*, Small Crown 4to, 1948.

L. M. BATES, *The Londoner's River*, Small 8vo, 1949.

K. RITTENER, *The River Thames*, Small Crown 4to, 1951.

H. PHILLIPS, *The Thames about 1750*, 4to, 1951.

J. IRWIN and J. HERBERT, *Sweete Themmes. An Anthology*, 1951.

GENERAL REFERENCE BOOKS

DEFOE's *Tour of Great Britain*, 3 vols., 8vo, 1724–27.

PERCY LUBBOCK, *Shades of Eton*, 1929.

SIR P. ABERCROMBIE, *Plan for Greater London*, 1944.

CELIA FIENNES, *Through England on a Side Saddle in the Days of William and Mary*, Large Crown 8vo, 1949.

Chapter One

LONDON RIVER:
SOUTHEND TO KEW BRIDGE

WHERE any great river runs down to the sea the precise point on its broad tidal estuary where river ends and sea begins can only be determined arbitrarily. It must inevitably consist merely of an imaginary boundary line, drawn by man for administrative convenience, across a desolate expanse of restless waters, glistening mudflats and marshes whose loneliness finds a voice in the crying and piping of seabirds and waders. So it is with the Thames.

For me, the real River Thames begins, or ends, at Teddington, where the jurisdiction of the Thames Conservancy commences and no tides ebb and flow. Below this point the great waterway assumes a character no less attractive but totally different; it becomes the Port of London or London River. Above Teddington is a river of pleasure whose broad tideless reaches are as carefully regulated, cleansed and controlled as the waters of an artificial lake in the grounds of some great estate. Below are the blackened, workaday and ever restless waters of London River, bounded, not by smooth lawns and riverside bungalows but by factories, warehouses, wharves and all that sprawling labyrinth of brick and stone and steel which composes the greatest city in the world. It was London River that created this stupendous agglomeration that is London, and it is a paradox that it should have itself remained less affected by the hand of man than the upper river. The movement of its dense commerce of merchant shipping, of lighters, barges and tugs is still determined by the eternal arbiter of its tides, and will continue to be so controlled unless the projected Thames Barrage ever becomes a reality.

Of the Teddington boundary there can be no doubt, but where, then, is the seaward limit of the Thames? Some say it is at Tilbury Fort (Figure 3), where the river men surrender downstream craft to the charge of the Channel Pilots. But perhaps it would be more accurate to say that the river ends at the limit of the jurisdiction of the Port of London Authority. That jurisdiction extends down the Essex bank as far as Havengore Creek, which, with the Rivers Roach and Crouch, forms the Island of Foulness. On the Kentish side the boundary is at Warden Point on the Isle of Sheppey, a line across the estuary from point to point passing almost midway between the Nore and Mouse Lightships.

I

Well within this boundary lie Southend and Leigh, both of which, when the nineteenth-century vogue for seaside resorts began, added 'on-Sea' to their names. Southend is to East London what Blackpool is to Lancashire, and no one would dispute its claim to be a seaside resort. It has everything that those who patronise such resorts have a right to expect except a good beach, and it proudly boasts the longest pier in the British Isles. At low water the sea deserts Southend, and at such a time this mile-long pier, striding over a great expanse of mudflats, seems to reflect a dogged determination on the part of the town to remain 'on-Sea' no matter what the cost. Over its girders an electric train rumbles purposefully seawards, as though to ensure that even the most indolent, senile or time-pressed visitor shall participate in this pursuit of a receding tide.

It is apparent from a map that Southend is in fact situated on the river estuary whereas, immediately east of the Port of London Authority boundary, the shore lines of Sheppey and of the Maplin Sands curve sharply south and north like the mouth of a funnel. Nevertheless, the estuary is four miles wide at high water off Southend, and haze or rain will obscure the Kentish coastline even from the pierhead. But in clear weather it is fascinating to stand on that pierhead and watch the commerce of the seven seas passing through Thames gate. A P. & O. liner, perhaps, outward bound from Tilbury; merchantmen of every port and nationality; grimy little colliers from the Tyne bringing, as their ancestors have done for centuries, 'sea-coal' to London. Now steam and diesel power have succeeded sail on the colliers, but we may still see the brown sails of a Thames barge (Figures 2, 3, 4), bound perhaps for Yarmouth, perhaps for some small wharf along the indented Essex coastline.

Beyond the smoke smudges of the shipping can be seen the coast of the Hundred of Hoo and the Isle of Sheppey. The stranger crossing to Sheppey over the Swale by Harty Ferry and walking northwards across the island would find it difficult to believe that such solitude and desolation could be found so near to London. His only company will be the sheep feeding on green and almost treeless levels intersected by dykes and punctuated by a few tiled and weatherboarded buildings. The rim of the sea-walls shuts out the sight of the sea but not the sound of it or the salt-laden wind. Even if he reaches Leysdown and takes the Isle of Sheppey light railway* home, the sense of remoteness will not leave him till he reaches Queensborough or Sheerness. The railway promotors, with the unquenchable optimism of their kind, planted the same seeds at Leysdown which produced such prolific growth at Southend. But, alas for their hopes, the soil of Sheppey did not suit them and only a small, weakly and slightly pathetic group of bungalows grew up. Instead of the railway 'developing' Sheppey, the island seems to have subdued the railway. The little train creeps apologetically across the island, stopping frequently as the guard descends to open and close the crossing-gates.

The Naval base of Sheerness commands the mouth of the River Medway which,

* The railway has been closed since the time of writing.

2   Gravesend from the Thames

From a drawing by S. Owen, engraved by R. G. Reeves, circa 1828

3   Tilbury Fort

From a drawing by S. Owen, engraved by R. G. Reeves, circa 1828

3

if the Port of London Authority boundary be accepted, is the last tributary of Thames. The river has gone down in history as the scene of the daring and successful Dutch raid upon the English fleet in Chatham Roads in the time of Charles II, but for centuries its waters have borne more peaceable and less dramatic traffic. At the time of the famous raid, the river was already serving the Kentish ironworks and bringing down timber from the Weald for use in the Naval dockyards. But navigation was difficult, obstructed by weirs and subject to protracted delays, until 1740 when the 'Company of Proprietors of the Navigation of the River Medway' was formed to make the river navigable to Tonbridge by boats of forty tons burden. Today, the smaller Medway sailing barges can trade to Tonbridge (Figure 7), but the ironworks and the great oaks are gone. Instead, cement works smudge the lower reaches of the river with their smoke and dust.

In the canal era the Thames & Medway Canal was built to facilitate the passage of traffic between the Medway towns and the Port of London. This involved cutting a tunnel nearly two miles long through the chalk spine of the Hundred of Hoo between Higham and Rochester. The canal was opened in 1824, but it was short-lived, for in 1846 the Gravesend & Rochester Railway Company was empowered to lay its metals through the tunnel. Today, you may still walk the towpath beside the canal's deserted waters from the entrance lock at Gravesend as far as Higham, where the railway, now electrified, swings into its bed.

The Isle of Grain forms the easterly tip of the Hundred of Hoo which divides Medway from Thames. Forlorn on its flat shore stands Port Victoria, another relic of nineteenth-century railway promoting optimism which, like Leysdown, failed to yield its expected harvest of traffic. The South Eastern Railway dreamed of competing with Queenborough and Harwich for the cross-Channel trade, and the fact that they proudly named their new port after the reigning sovereign reveals the height of their aspiration. Alas, they came to nothing, although a night service was operated until 1904. Today, the shuttle service on the Hundred of Hoo Branch uses the new line to All-Hallows-on-Sea, and only two trains a day penetrate to Port Victoria, not to connect with any 'swift packet', but to perform the more mundane task of conveying its few inhabitants to and from their work.

Though the Thames is still half a mile wide at Gravesend it has already assumed the character of a great river rather than an estuary, while it has never occurred to the inhabitants of Gravesend (Figure 2) to claim for their town the appellation 'on-Sea'. Yet in one sense there is a more authentic atmosphere of the sea at Gravesend than is to be found at Leigh or Southend. The popularity of seaside resorts may wax and wane with little effect upon the life of the sea, whereas Gravesend continues, as it has done for centuries to play its part in that workaday world of sea-going traffic. On the waterfront are the short pier and stage where the Tilbury Ferry steamers berth, the headquarters of the Channel and River or 'mud' pilots who here exchange responsibilities, and the Customs House whose officers board the liners which dock at Tilbury. Here, too, is the small 'Fishermen's Church'

2*

of St. Andrew. These institutions form part of an agglomeration of buildings old and new which, though individually possessing no great beauty or architectural merit, collectively combine to distil that peculiar and fascinating atmosphere which seems to be characteristic of mercantile waterfronts the world over. Many of the older houses are built of that dingy yellow brick, which, though indigenous, is perhaps the least prepossessing of regional building materials. Above them rises the lantern tower of Gravesend Church (Figure 2), an eighteenth-century building which enshrines the memory of the ill-fated Princess Pocahontas. This tower is the first or last English landmark for those whom the great liners bear between Tilbury and the ends of the earth.

It was at Tilbury Fort that Elizabeth delivered her famous speech of defiance in the face of Spain's Armada. But there is little of old Tilbury to be seen now except the little inn called the 'World's End' and the noble seventeenth-century Watergate of the Fort which bears in its pediment the Stuart arms (Figure 3). Instead, Tilbury, with its hotel and railway station and its huge docks with their vistas of stork-like cranes, has become the water-gate of modern London. Until 1930 liner passengers had to be conveyed to or from Tilbury by tender, but in May of that year the immense floating landing stage, 80 feet wide and over 1,000 feet long, was opened to obviate the need for tenders. The *Mauretania,* the largest vessel that has ever entered the Thames, successfully berthed at Tilbury's stage.

Few people realise that practically the whole course of the Thames between Richmond and the sea has been determined and prescribed by man. The prehistoric embryo of the greatest city in the world was a small settlement on the rising ground where St. Paul's Cathedral stands, protected on all sides by the Thames, the Fleet and by marshland. Eastwards, a great estuary spread seawards, at high tide a waste of waters, at low water a desolate expanse of sand, mudflats and saltmarsh. We tacitly accept London River as a part of the natural topography of our island, but if some ancient ancestor of ours could return from the mists of this remote past he would appreciate what a stupendous work of reclamation had been accomplished. Generations of men of many races laboured at this task; the Belgæ; the Romans; the Normans; the Italians Acontius and Baptiste Castilione in the time of Henry VIII; the Dutchman Cornelius Vermuyden, better known for his work in the Fens, and last but not least the redoubtable Captain Perry of Rodborough in Gloucestershire. The long history of the work is by no means one of steady progress. Often the conjunction of an easterly gale with a high spring tide would lend the imprisoned river a giant's strength; its waters would seek out some weak or neglected part of man's defences, breach it, and undo the work of centuries. There were serious breaches at Erith on the south bank and at Limehouse on the north bank in the sixteenth and seventeenth centuries, the former being eventually closed by the Italians already mentioned. When the Limehouse breach occurred in 1676, the waters swept over the Isle of Dogs and along the line of the present West India Docks. By so doing they short-circuited the great southerly loop which

4

4   Greenwich Hospital from the River

From a drawing by S. Owen, engraved by R. G. Reeves, circa 1828

5   Greenwich Hospital from the Park Hill looking towards London

From the watercolour by John Dobbin, signed and dated 1851

In the possession of Messrs. Frank T. Sabin, Park House, Rutland Gate, S.W.7

the river makes in the direction of Deptford and Greenwich, and had it not been for the fact that Deptford was already established as a Naval Dockyard the breach might never have been closed and the river held to this new and more direct course.

But it was the north bank in the vicinity of Barking and Dagenham which proved the most difficult to secure, and which was the scene of the last major struggle between man and the waters of Thames. Vermuyden had successfully closed a serious breach near Dagenham which occurred about 1621, and which flooded the Dagenham and Havering Levels. In the course of this work Vermuyden embanked Dagenham Creek and closed its outfall by a wooden sluice or 'clow' which released the waters of the creek at low tide, but excluded the Thames at high water. Vermuyden's sluice was subsequently neglected, however, and in 1707 it blew up under the pressure of an exceptionally high tide. So the levels were submerged once again. Various unsuccessful attempts were made to stop the gap by sinking old ships filled with ballast, or by constructing a series of enormous wooden trunks which were filled with chalk. Samuel Smiles, in his *Lives of the Engineers,* tells the amusing story of how the force of the tide lifted one of these trunks, spilling its contents, and floating it away. It drifted down river on the ebb, pursued along the bank by a distraught local landowner crying fruitlessly: "Stop her! Oh, stop her!" Its appearance at Gravesend occasioned no little alarm and consternation amongst the assembled shipping, but it sailed by harmlessly and eventually stranded on a sandbank at the Nore. These obstructions only served to make matters worse, for the waters undermined and surrounded them, so that when Captain Perry at last undertook to close the breach in 1715 he was confronted with a formidable gulf 50 feet deep at low water. Perry, however, was a man of great resource and with technical abilities that were years in advance of his time. His first step was to make two additional openings, controlled by sluices, in the embankment. In this way he reduced the flow of water through the breach. He then commenced to close the gap with interlocking oak piling, protecting the piles by throwing down quantities of clay. There were many set-backs and difficulties, for as the piles advanced so the force of the water through the narrowing gap increased. At last, however, after five years work by three hundred men, the last pile was driven and the last serious breach in the Thames defences closed. Perry subsequently enclosed his piling in a clay bank which was 25 feet high and 25 to 30 feet broad at the base.

All this centuries'-long labour of confining the Thames had a two-fold object; firstly the conversion of marshes into rich farmland, and secondly the improvement of the river as a commercial highway. Upon the achievement of this second object the commercial life of London still depends, but our civilisation no longer recognises the primary importance of the first objective. Most of the land which our forefathers laboured to reclaim from the waste has become waste once more—a waste of bricks and mortar, of tarmac, steel and concrete; sterile crops which yield a greater profit than corn and pasture. They will continue to flourish until man is forcibly and painfully reminded of the fact that while he may not be able to live by bread alone, he certainly cannot live without it.

Between Gravesend and Woolwich the man-made desolation is more sterile and sombre than any primæval salt marsh. The once fertile flat lands bordering the river have become London's backyard; the harsh reality behind the glittering façade, which neither eyes nor nose can ignore. All the way up the Long Reach and beyond it the factories sprawl, tall pylons and fuming chimneys pricking the wide skies; soap factories; cement works; oil storage depots; explosives factories; the great Ford plant at Dagenham behind which there still survives the lake formed by the breach of 1707. These factories are interspersed by dreary stretches of marshland as yet 'undeveloped', and by vast refuse dumps, smouldering, noisome and rat infested. Finally, as Woolwich is approached, come Barking Power Station and the enormous, reeking plant of the London Gas Light and Coke Company at Beckton. Nearby, the main southern and northern outfall sewers pour the vast sum of London's drainage system into the river; a noisome burden, but at the same time a waste of fertility staggering to contemplate. In the midst of all this a few pathetic relics of the pre-industrial age survive; the thirteenth-century parish church of West Thurrock dwarfed by a new seven-storey soap factory, or the lovely little church of Stone, surrounded by cement works and smothered in their dust, whose Early English vaulting and foliated stonework is said to have been the work of one of the architects of Westminster Abbey. So wide is the rift which industrialism has forced between us and our past that these ancient buildings seems as far removed from their modern surroundings as the monoliths of Avebury or the long barrows of the Downs.

Standing on Shooter's Hill above Woolwich in 1697, Celia Fiennes described the prospect as: ". . . A vast tract of ground, which appears in the greatest variety, some lands cloathed with trees, others with grass and flowers, gardens, orchards, with all sorts of herbage and tillage, with severall little towns all by the river." One wonders what comment she would make if she could return to the same vantage point today.

Perhaps the most interesting feature of modern Woolwich, particularly in these days when all is measured in money value, is its Free Ferry. Operated by the London County Council since 1889, it is, so far as I am aware, the only free public transport service in this country. Plying between South Woolwich and North Woolwich, it is well patronised, because it affords the only regular river crossing for vehicles as well as foot passengers between the Blackwall tunnel and the railway ferry service at Tilbury. For fifteen hours a day four ferry boats, two in service and two in reserve, maintain a twelve-minute service. They are curious craft, 166 feet long and with an immense beam of 44 feet which enables them to carry 100 tons of vehicles and 1,000 passengers on a draught of only 4 feet 9 inches. With large independently driven feathering paddle wheels and tall funnels fore and aft of the raised vehicle deck, they present an unwieldy and archaic appearance reminiscent of the stern-

6

6 The Thames at Deptford

From a watercolour by Samuel Scott, circa 1760

In the collection of William Hartmann, Esq.

wheeled 'show-boats' of the Mississippi. However, one has only to observe the way in which the ferry boats thread their way through the river traffic and come up to the landing stages on a tidal current which may be running at anything up to eight knots, to realise that appearances are deceptive and that they are in fact extremely manœvrable.

The 'finest hour' of the Free Ferry Service was on the night of September 7th 1940, when wave after wave of German bombers flew in to bomb London's dockland by the light of the great fires they had started before darkness fell. The inhabitants of the mean streets of Silvertown found themselves cut off by fire from escape northwards, and throughout that dreadful night the ferry-boat *Squires* shuttled resolutely to and fro conveying load after load of refugees across to the south bank.

Near the Free-Ferry crossing there is a tunnel for pedestrians under the river which was opened in 1912. On the one occasion when I traversed it I thought its architecture and atmosphere reminiscent of a public lavatory, so that the fact that more people cross the river by this gloomy tunnel than by the ferry seems a curious comment on our seafaring race. Perhaps the answer is that in an age of feverish time-saving, many people feel they cannot afford the few extra minutes required for a free voyage in the open air.

The great Royal docks, Victoria, Albert and George Vth, form the northern boundary of Silvertown and North Woolwich, and together total the greatest still-water dock area in the world. Close to the western entrance to Victoria Dock is the older East India Dock, part of which is now being swept away to make room for a new power station. This dock has ancestral associations for me, because in the seventeenth century John Rolt of Blackwall owned a shipbuilding yard here, a connection with the life of the river which is perpetuated on the south bank by Rolt Street in Deptford. It would seem that the maritime interests of the family were not confined merely to shipbuilding, but extended to the East India Company, for another contemporary representative, Sir Thomas, is described as 'President of India' in his epitaph in the little church of Sacombe in Hertfordshire. John, sad to relate, speculated in 'the South Sea Bubble' and was forced to sell his shipyard as a result.

Close by East India Dock the tortuous Bow Creek enters the Thames. This is the old natural mouth of the River Lea, whose history as a navigation to Hertford is as old as that of the Medway to Tonbridge. Under the River Lea Navigation Improvement Act of 1766 Limehouse Cut was constructed to give the river a more direct outlet to the Thames near Regent's Canal Dock, Limehouse. In 1769 the Lea's main tributary, the Stort, was made navigable by Sir George Duckett, two loaded barges from London arriving at Bishop's Stortford in October of that year. In 1824 his son, Sir George Duckett II, also made a contribution to the navigable waterways of the Thames basin in the shape of the short Hertford Union Canal, which links the Lea with the Regent's Canal at Old Ford. For a reason that is obscure and on the face of it somewhat unfair, this useful little waterway became known for many years as 'Duckett's Folly'.

After miles of industrial squalor the magnificent river frontage of Greenwich Hospital (Figure 4) (as it is still commonly called) is balm to the eye of the up-river traveller. Nowhere else is the waterside of Thames—or any other English river—graced by a display of English Renaissance architecture of such Venetian splendour. Vanbrugh, Hawksmoor, Campbell and Ripley all made their contributions to Greenwich, but the lion's share of the credit is due to Inigo Jones, his pupil John Webb and, above all, Sir Christopher Wren.

There was once a Tudor Palace at Greenwich, of which only a vaulted undercroft remains. The first building of a new palace projected by the Stuarts was the Queen's House, designed by Inigo Jones for Anne of Austria and subsequently occupied by Queen Henrietta Maria. It is difficult to believe that this example of pure Renaissance architecture was a product of Jacobean England. It was not until the Restoration that the next addition to the palace was built by John Webb, to the designs of Inigo Jones, on the riverfront on the upstream side of the Queen's House. Building was interrupted in 1669, and by the time it was recommenced in 1696 it had been decided that the buildings, together with projected additions, should become a hospital for seamen, Sir Christopher Wren being appointed architect. It is a significant paradox that whereas in this so-called 'century of the common man' public buildings of this type have a bleak gracelessness which is excused by the convenient word 'functional', Wren's design for Greenwich Hospital reveals, in its regal magnificence, a qualitative integrity which no change of function could deflect. Had he been called upon to build an abattoir or a public lavatory, one feels that this peer of English architects would have lavished upon his designs the same exacting craftsmanship.

At Greenwich, Wren welded the work of his predecessors into one splendid composition. He completed the block begun to Inigo Jones' design, built another in exact facsimile on the downstream side and added to the rear of each a new building. These, known as the William and Mary blocks, face each other across the broad vista between the two ranges which run down from the Queen's House to the river's edge. Down the sides of this vista between his new buildings and the Queen's House, Wren set twin colonnades of coupled Doric columns, each crowned by a dome. His design therefore consists of two matching but separate ranges. The fact that it is Inigo Jones' original building which forms the centre piece and focal point linking cupola, column and pediment in one harmonious whole, seems an inspired gesture on the part of Wren towards his great predecessor.

The buildings continued to serve their purpose as a Royal Hospital until 1873. They are now occupied by the Royal Naval College and the National Maritime Museum, which constitutes a superbly housed and maintained visual record of English seafaring history.

Deptford Creek, actually the mouth of the Ravensbourne, divides Greenwich

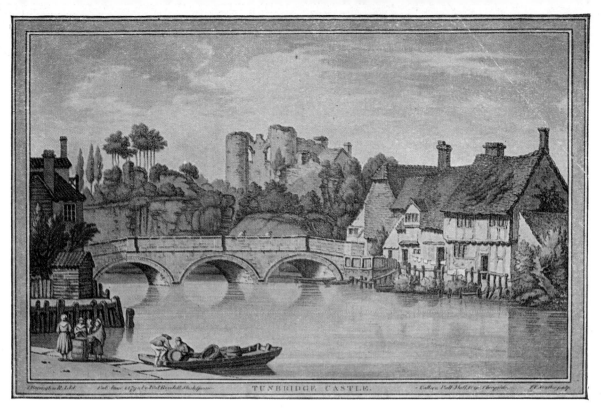

7   The Castle and River Medway, Tonbridge, Kent, in 1795

From a drawing by J. Farington, R.A., engraved by J. C. Stadler

8   The Tower of London in 1795

From a drawing by J. Farington, R.A., engraved by J. C. Stadler

from Deptford, where Henry VIII established the Royal Dockyard which was the birthplace of the English Navy. By the end of the seventeenth century fighting-ships had so increased in size that the Royal Yards were moved further downstream to Woolwich. The Royal Victualling Yard remains at Deptford, but the dock has become the foreign cattle market. It was here that Evelyn discovered an unknown and impoverished young wood carver and, impressed by the quality of his craftsmanship, recommended him to Charles II. His name was Grinling Gibbons.

With the exception of its two churches of St. Nicholas and St. Paul, modern Deptford has effectually succeeded in obliterating most of the visual evidence of its historic past. Figure 6 shows Deptford very much as Evelyn and Pepys must have known it, an attractive riverside village of Kentish tile and weatherboarding.

Upstream from Deptford is Limehouse Reach and the heart of Dockland; Millwall and West India Docks on the Isle of Dogs, and the Surrey Commercial Docks in Rotherhithe on the south bank. A little beyond them is the mouth of Limehouse Cut and the entrance to Regent's Canal Dock which, via the Regent's Canal, links London River with the whole network of the canal system. Here small steamers or lighters may be seen discharging cargoes of steel or copper into the long, narrow canal craft for shipment to the Midlands. Greenland Dock, on the Surrey side, also has its canal which, under the high sounding title of the Grand Surrey, was originally projected to run from the Thames to Epsom, though in the Act of 1801 Mitcham was to be its destination. The optimistic engineer, one Ralph Dodd, even planned to extend it to Kingston and the River Wey. In the event, the canal progressed no further than Camberwell, though the short-lived Croydon Canal was connected to it. With the numerous wharves on its banks, the short waterway was virtually an extended dock, and the canal proprietors did, in fact, turn themselves into a Dock Company which was eventually absorbed by the Port of London Authority.

In view of the pre-eminence of London as a port, it is a surprising fact that although there were considerable enclosed wet docks at Liverpool in the eighteenth century, practically no such accommodation for shipping was provided in the Port of London until the turn of that century. There were only a few very small private docks and the original Greenland Dock which, as its name indicates, was used entirely by whalers. Merchandise was handled almost exclusively at riverside quays. This meant that all but the smallest ships must anchor in the river and make use of open lighters to land or ship their cargoes, so that a contemporary writer described the Thames between London Bridge and Blackwall as "a double forest of masts with a narrow avenue in mid-channel". Figure 9, though engraved about 1828, indicates that a great volume of shipping still anchored in the river at that time.

The universal system of lighterage encouraged pilfering on an enormous scale, and it was in the attempt to check this that the Thames Police Force was established in 1798. The efforts of this Force had little effect, and it was realised that the only true remedy lay in the provision of enclosed wet docks surrounded by warehouses and capable of accommodating the largest ships. To this end the greatest civil engineering talents of the day were employed. William Jessop, pupil of Smeaton and engineer of many canals, was the first in the field, constructing the West India Dock which was opened in 1802. Shortly after him came John Rennie, engineer of the London Docks (1805) and the East India Dock (1806), while Thomas Telford built St. Katherine's, the nearest dock to the City, which was opened in October 1828. Throughout the nineteenth century additional docks were constructed to cope with increasing commerce and to accommodate larger ships. The last dock to be built belongs to our century, the King George Vth, opened in 1921.

Generations of 'thriller' writers have invested the names of London's dockland, Wapping, Shadwell, Limehouse and the Isle of Dogs, with a forbidding flavour which no harsh reality can eradicate. Limehouse is full of sinister Chinese with inscrutable almond eyes, while its opium dens, each 'furnished with oriental splendour' seem to be as numerous as its pubs. There can scarcely be a grimy warehouse in Shadwell or Wapping that has not at some fictional period concealed the luxurious apartment of some master criminal provided, needless to say, with a trapdoor for the convenient discharge into the river of bound and gagged victims. The author chiefly responsible for indulging my youthful fantasies about London's dockland was Mr. Sax Rohmer. Avidly I followed the indefatigable Nayland Smith as he pursued that yellow peril Doctor Fu Manchu and the seductive Karamaneh through several volumes. Even at that gullible age I wondered why the Doctor, who displayed so much devilish ingenuity in devising complicated traps and tortures for Nayland Smith, was guileless enough to keep Karamaneh in his entourage. For she had a soft spot for the detective, and unfailingly came to his rescue when all else failed. On these occasions her providential appearance was invariably heralded by a perfume described as 'elusive', but which seems to have been strong enough to overpower the most potent of dockland stenches.

The dockland of fact is very different from this dockland of fiction, but, like the environs of every seaport, it has its authentic magic, particularly after nightfall, when pitiless daylight no longer emphasises the murkiness of water or the drabness of smoke-blackened brick. Then innumerable lights, mirrored by the water in wavering, serpentine reflections or blurred by drifting steam or smoke like the moon by cloud-wrack, reveal only in dark silhouette irregular roofs, tall chimneys and the poised jibs of the cranes. No one has distilled this midnight magic more effectually into words than Wilfred Owen in his poem 'Shadwell Stair':

> I am the ghost of Shadwell Stair,
>   Along the wharves by the water-house,
>   And through the dripping slaughter-house,
> I am the shadow that walks there.
>
> Yet I have flesh both firm and cool,
>   And eyes tumultuous as the gems
>   Of moons and lamps in the lapping Thames
> When dusk sails wavering down the pool.

9   The Custom House and Shipping in the Upper Pool

From a drawing by S. Owen, engraved by R. G. Reeves, circa 1828

Shuddering the purple street-arc burns
  Where I watch always; from the banks
  Dolorously the shipping clanks,
And after me a strange tide turns.

I walk till the stars of London wane
  And dawn creeps up the Shadwell Stair.
  But when the crowing syrens blare
I with another ghost am lain.'

There is one name in dockland which carries with it very different associations, evoking the memory of London's river as it was in the days before industrialism, when pleasure and commerce were compatible partners. This is Cherry Gardens Pier on the south bank opposite the London Docks. "And so to the Cherry Garden, and then by water singing finely to the bridge and there landed." So writes Pepys, conjuring for us in one sentence the vision of a green shade and the echo of voices from a past that in our sombre world seems as remote as Eden. No doubt Robert Herrick, too, knew the Cherry Garden. When he returned to Devonshire from Westminster in 1662, he was moved to write the nostalgic poem 'His Teares to Thamasis', which reveals the pleasures which Londoners once derived from their river:—

'. . . No more shall I reiterate thy Strand,
Whereon so many Stately Structures stand:
Nor in the summer's sweeter evenings go
To bathe in thee (as thousand others doe,)
No more shall I along thy christall glide,
In Barge (with boughs and rushes beautified)
With soft-smooth virgins (for our chaste disport)
To Richmond, Kingstone, and to Hampton-Court:
Never againe shall I with Finnie-Ore
Put from, or draw unto the faithfull shore:
And Landing here, or safely Landing there,
Make way to my beloved Westminster:
Or to the Golden-cheap-side, where the earth
Of Julia Herrick gave me to my birth.'

For years Sir Alan Herbert has endeavoured to educate Londoners to make more use of their river, and the recent introduction of a 'water-bus' service is a step in that direction. But its patrons can never enjoy the beauty that Pepys and Herrick knew, and the Cherry Garden, like the later gardens of Vauxhall and Cremorne, survives in name alone.

True ornament is the natural expression of the craftsman's joy and pride in his work, and because it is true we see it as a homogeneous part of the work itself so that it is often difficult to say where function ends and ornament begins. Ornament is false veneer if it becomes mere ostentation, the expression of man's pride in himself rather than in his work, or a means of disguising work of whose quality or function man feels ashamed. Ornament became debased in this way in the Victorian age, and the reaction against such excesses has taken the form of a bleak and joyless 'functionalism' which, while it abjures Victorian vices, possesses little or no positive virtue. Perhaps it is this negative quality in the architecture of our own day which makes us admire some of the greater works of the Victorians. In them a great tradition may have become false and overblown, but at least they exhibit a superb self-confidence, and he is a purist indeed who can travel the river without sparing a second glance for Barry's Houses of Parliament or for the Tower Bridge. The bridge is architecturally false in that it is simply a great piece of mechanism, designed by Sir J. Wolfe Barry, camouflaged by a certain Horace Jones in a shell of 'Gothic' stonework. Yet, seeing the tall twin towers which dominate the Upper Pool, one is compelled to sympathise with the conception of making this machine appear as a great pseudo-mediæval gateway and drawbridge to the City of London rather than a mere mass of functional steelwork. And what a machine it is! Whereas the majority of our modern engineering marvels leave me strangely unmoved, the engineer in me is fascinated by the sight of the enormous bascules of the Tower Bridge as they rise swiftly and easily upward to admit the passage of a ship through the Pool. Perhaps this is because our mechanical marvels are essentially machines built by machines, products of minutely specialised ingenuity which lack that human touch of practical and versatile engineering craftsmanship upon which the designer of the Tower Bridge manifestly relied.

Just above Tower Bridge stands the Tower itself (Figure 8), its moat and bastions symbolically defended by the rows of ancient cannon ranged along Tower Wharf. The meticulous preservation of this most celebrated of secular historical buildings seems to have bestowed upon it an air of unreality. The sight of a Beefeater pacing beneath walls so carefully scoured and pointed creates the impression that the building must be a film studio illusion and not truly a great fortress dating back to the time of William the Conqueror. Above the Tower, on Tower Hill, stand the Royal Mint, the bomb-gutted shell of the eighteenth-century Trinity House, whose Brethren guard our coastwise lights, and the great twentieth-century block of the Port of London Authority offices.

Bestriding the Upper Pool is London Bridge, the first (or last) fixed bridge over the Thames, the most celebrated and probably the oldest river crossing. For the first London Bridge is believed to have been a wooden structure built by the monks of St. Mary of Southwark seventy-five years before the Norman Conquest. The first stone bridge—Old London Bridge as it came to be called—was built about 1209 and survived until the second decade of the nineteenth century. It became lined with buildings on both sides (see Figure 11) so that its thoroughfare resembled a narrow street, and its longevity is the more remarkable in view of the immense burden thus placed upon its piers. Beneath a number of its narrow arches waterwheels were set

12

which harnessed the ebb and flow of the tides to pump the City's water supply. The power available must indeed have been considerable, for the massive piers and the pilings or 'starlings' which protected them so obstructed the river that a fall of five feet was produced when the tide was running strongly, a circumstance scarcely calculated to assist navigation. By the middle of the eighteenth century the condition of the bridge gave cause for alarm, and the opening of the New Westminster bridge designed by the Swiss engineer Labelye in 1749 served to emphasis the shortcomings of the older structure. On Labelye's advice all the buildings on the bridge were demolished in 1758, the great central pier was removed and a new arch turned to replace the two previously existing. This last alteration was ill advised, for it caused the river to scour and to undermine the adjacent piers. Moreover, the new arch, by liberating the pent-up waters, robbed the waterwheels of much of their power and so threatened London's water supply. An alarmed City Council summoned John Smeaton to their aid, and as a result of his recommendations tons of stonework from the recently demolished City gates were dumped into the river to protect the piers and to restore the head of water to the wheels. By this means the life of the old bridge was prolonged for another sixty years.

By the turn of the century, engineers and architects were experimenting with a new material—cast iron. Of this medium Thomas Telford was the greatest master. Already he had built a number of cast-iron bridges in Shropshire, while his great canal aqueduct over the Dee at Vron Cysyllte was nearing completion. On the strength of these achievements, Telford produced a design for a new London Bridge of cast iron which, perhaps more than any of his accomplished works, gives us the measure of Telford's greatness as an engineer. He proposed to bridge the river by a single arch of 600-feet span giving a clear headway above high water of 65 feet, the roadway to be 45 feet wide at the crown and double that width at the abutments. Though it was estimated that the arch would contain 6,500 tons of ironwork, the effect of the design is one of soaring grace and lightness. Even today such a conception seems stupendous, so that it might be thought that in 1801 it would have been dismissed as an impracticable dream. On the contrary, a committee appointed to investigate the scheme reached the conclusion that it was practicable. A bridge of such headway, however, involved lengthy approach ramps which would have occupied much valuable riverside property, and it was mainly for this reason that Telford's design was abandoned. So the ancient bridge continued to stand until 1831, when the New London Bridge designed by John Rennie was opened thirty yards further upstream. Rennie had already bridged London river at Waterloo and Southwark, but this, his last design, is generally considered his finest work in bridge building. The engineer died soon after the design was submitted, and the work was carried out under the supervision of his son, Sir John Rennie. The bridge is of Cornish and Scottish granite except for the underwater masonry, which is sandstone grit quarried at Bramley Fall, near Leeds. Figure 10, from a watercolour of 1830, shows Rennie's bridge nearing completion. Beneath its arches can be seen the old bridge in its final form.

Canaletto's well-known picture of the Thames from Old Somerset House (Figure 12) is undoubtedly somewhat idealised. At no time could the river frontage have presented quite so regular a perspective and so smooth a symmetry. Did London River ever look like this, even in 1747? It is doubtful. This air of unreality is heightened by the picture's lighting. Cloudless sky, river front and smooth light-flecked water bask in a breathless golden heat haze which belongs, not to London but to the artist's native Venice. Nevertheless, William Wordsworth's equally well-known poem, composed on Labelye's Westminster bridge in 1803, reveals that even at this later date the poet's eye saw a picture that was not dissimilar in the fresher, clearer light of an early-morning sun. It is tempting to speculate what artist and poet would make of the long vista of modern London that unfolds before the water traveller between London Bridge and Putney. Earth may now have other things to show more fair, but scarcely anywhere else in the world can the hand of man have wrought so fantastic a mixture of beauty and ugliness, pomp and squalor, of architectural dignity and vulgar pretension. Here are still the 'ships, towers, domes, theatres and temples' which Wordsorth catalogues, but to them have been added modern temples of commerce and power such as the immense concrete block of Shell-Mex house reared over the ruin of the Adams' Adelphi, or the fuming power stations of Battersea and Lott's Road with their towering chimneys. Here is architecture of every style, period and merit; Sir William Chambers' Somerset House; the ancient castellated pile of Lambeth Palace; Wren's stately Chelsea Hospital; Norman Shaw's 'Franco-Scottish Baronial' New Scotland Yard; the seven execrable Victorian blocks of St. Thomas's Hospital. The contrast between bank and bank is often extreme. From the comparative order and dignity of the Grosvenor Embankment the windows of the vast modern warren of flats at Dolphin Square gaze across the water at the chaotic commercial jungle of Nine Elms and Vauxhall. It is hard indeed to believe that there was once the fashionable New Spring Garden beloved by 'Prinny'.

Since the days of Carlyle, of Meredith, Rossetti, Swinburne and Whistler, Chelsea has been beloved of those who follow art for art's sake, so that its name now seems inextricably associated with those who regard unconventional appearance and behaviour as a conventional and essential qualification for intellectual pursuits. Chelsea's riverside windows are more favoured than those of Dolphin Square in that they look across to Battersea Park which, flanked by the only two suspension bridges over London River, is the only sizeable oasis on the South Bank.

To all who love craftsmanship the names of Chelsea and Battersea mean neither art nor power stations but fine porcelain and exquisite enamel. The two workshops (it seems an insult to call them factories) almost faced each other across the river. I suspect that the small open penthouse and oven which appears in Samuel Scott's watercolour (*circa* 1760) of the Thames at Battersea (Figure 13) may well depict

14

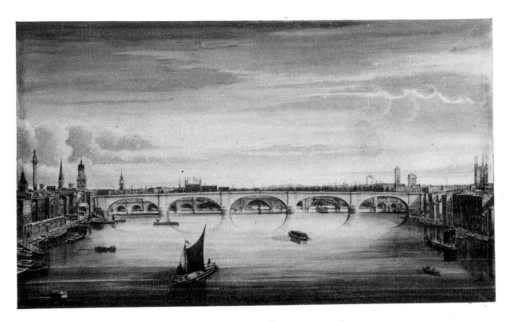

10   New London Bridge, opened 1831

From a watercolour by G. Yates, 1830

11   Old London Bridge, demolished 1757

From a watercolour by T. M. Baynes, 1824

the birthplace of Battersea enamel as it looked at that time. Price's candleworks now occupy its site.

Next above the Albert Suspension Bridge comes Battersea Bridge, Bazalgette's Victorian successor to the old wooden bridge which Whistler immortalised in his famous 'Nocturne'. The old bridge may have gone, rapacious development and the bombs of the second world war may have scarred or swept away much of the London that Whistler knew, yet when dusk falls the old magic that he saw and painted still returns to the riverside he loved.

I have to confess that I am no lover of London; I become too easily overwhelmed by the hectic pace of the City, by its crowds, its traffic, its noise and its smells, which batter the five senses into insensibility by gorging them with more than they can possibly assimilate. I am oppressed and imprisoned, too, by the thought that miles of pavement and of bricks and mortar hem me in. Were I to die in London, I would, I know, like Falstaff, babble of green fields. The London parks can bring only the illusion of relief from such sickness, for there is a certain melancholy air of unreality in these islands of green which survive on sufferance in a man-made desert. They no longer seem quite natural. But no matter how its waters may be confined and polluted or its banks disfigured, the river's quality of natural and eternal freedom cannot be destroyed. It is only by or on the river, particularly when dusk falls or in the night time, that it is possible in spirit to step aside from the fume and fret of London and find solace. The crowds, the ceaseless surge of the streets, the trains that roar with flashes of blue fire across the river, all are enslaved to the hands that creep over the yellow moon-face of the Westminster Clock. Could we but watch those hands quicken from a crawl to a spin, we would see the pulse of London quicken with them like an accelerated cinema film, see the traffic become a whirling nebula of light, see buildings fall and others rise. Yet, though the city vanish and leave no wrack behind, the river would still flow on as always, its waters eternally renewed yet eternally the same.

> 'And something said that far away, over the hills and far away,
> There came a crawling thunder and the end of all things here.'

So wrote G. K. Chesterton in the apocalyptic poem which he sub-titled 'On the Embankment in Stormy Weather'. It would seem that he, too, was moved by the symbolic contrast between the temporal and the eternal which city and river present.

Hurlingham and Ranelagh have fallen on evil days. They seem destined either to become public spaces or to disappear like their predecessors at Vauxhall and Cremorne. By the same token, part of the grounds of Fulham Palace have become allotments. Opposite Fulham Palace and upstream of Putney Bridge, where the boat race starts, the Thames towpath begins, continuing, with certain interruptions and numerous river crossings, all the way to Inglesham.

Once past the Ranelagh Club grounds, the Surrey bank of Barnes is mainly devoted to the Metropolitan Waterboard. But after passing under Hammersmith

Bridge, the North bank rewards the traveller with the gracious riverside terraces of Hammersmith and Chiswick. The associations of riverside Hammersmith are with fine printing, for 'The Doves' by Hammersmith bridge became the imprint of Cobden–Sanderson's Press, while little more than a stone's throw away on the Upper Mall is Kelmscott House where, in 1890, William Morris began to produce his even more famous Kelmscott Press books. Morris named the house after his Oxfordshire Manor, and twice he journeyed by water between the two Kelmscotts.

Off Chiswick Mall is Chiswick Ait, first of the numerous Thames islets. All these islands are known as 'Aits', though I have not encountered the term on any other river. The Oxford Dictionary conjectures that it may derive from the old English 'Iggath', though such a derivation seems hard to credit. Traditionally, Chiswick Ait was once a 'cranoge' or prehistoric Lake settlement, of the Glaston-bury type, and at a later period of history a camping place for Danish raiders. Erosion has since seriously diminished its size, and unless it is protected from the scour of the tides it may eventually disappear.

Beyond Chiswick Ait the second of the great loops which the river makes between Putney and Kew Bridge encloses a peninsula of playing fields and open spaces which was once a great osier bed. Its present name of the 'Duke's Meadows' commemorates its ownership by the Dukes of Devonshire who succeeded that Earl of Burlington who inherited Chiswick House from the Somersets and rebuilt it in the Palladian style in 1730.

Even central London cannot produce a greater contrast than the north bank of the Thames above and below Kew Bridge. Above lies the squalid, smoky, workaday waterfront of Brentford, dominated by its huge gasworks; below is Strand-on-the-Green, perhaps the loveliest surviving Thames-side terrace in all London. Only a pavement separates the gracious, irregular row of Georgian houses from the steeply sloping foreshore. Here, unlike other parts of Thames-side London, the ravages of war have been rapidly and skilfully made good, and the only discordant note is provided by the trains of the District Railway which rattle and rumble over the river on their ugly iron bridge. In one of the loveliest of the houses on the Strand lived the painter Zoffany. Now he lies buried across the water, near his greater pre-decessor, Gainsborough, in the graveyard of the Queen Anne church on Kew Green. Despite their proximity to the roaring traffic of Kew Bridge, the old houses of Strand-on-the Green and Kew Green seem to remain curiously aloof, jealously guarding the atmosphere of a more spacious and less hurried age.

12 An Eighteenth-Century View of the Thames, painted by Caneletto, looking East from the Gardens of Old Somerset House

In the Royal Collection. Reproduced by Gracious Permission of His Majesty The King

Chapter Two

BRENTFORD TO WINDSOR

THE name of the ancient county borough of Brentford commemorates the ford by which the Roman road from London to Bath crossed the River Brent, which flows down to the Thames from its source near Mill Hill on the Hertfordshire border. There is also said to have been a prehistoric ford across the Thames at Brentford. Here, it was once asserted, Julius Cæsar forced the river crossing, but archæologists now believe Coway Stakes, near Walton, to be a more probable site, and the granite column at Brentford which commemorated the event has been removed. There have been later battles at Brentford which rest on surer historical foundations, the last being that which accompanied the Royalist occupation of Syon House during the Civil War.

Though battles bulk large in history books, they seldom or never have a very great or lasting effect upon the social history of a region. They are, at most, violent interruptions of a course in the determination of which local topography is by far the most important factor. Thus the history of Brentford and its varying fortunes have been linked through the ages with the river and with the great Bath Road which passes through its High Street. Brentford's fortunes grew with the traffic of the road, the culminating point being reached when Beau Nash reigned at Bath and the long High Street was renowned for the number of its inns and posting houses. The building of railways caused an eclipse, but the coming of the internal combustion engine, though it did not restore to Brentford the prosperity of coaching days, produced a spate of traffic which proved too much for the narrow High Street. It was accordingly by-passed by the Great West Road, although today the town seems to have become as congested as ever, for many heavy commercial vehicles appear to prefer the old route to the Great West with its numerous traffic lights.

The decline of the road in the Railway Age was offset by the effect of the Grand Junction Canal, which was opened throughout in 1805, and which considerably increased the importance of Brentford as an inland port. From the foot of the flight of locks at Hanwell to the Thames, the canal constructors canalised the Brent and used its waters to supply the large dock basin where merchandise brought by lighter from the Port of London is transhipped into canal boats. Not all the traffic from the Port is transhipped, however. The bulky barge loads of esparto grass, which have

17

become a common sight on London River, are hauled by horses up the canal from Brentford direct to their destination at the big paper mills at Croxley and Apsley in Hertfordshire.

Seen from Kew Gardens, the waterfront of Brentford opposite, part screened by a chain of willowy aits, looks shabby and unprepossessing, as indeed it is. But like all waterside areas it has its odd corners which repay investigation. It is fascinating, for example, to leave the busy High Street for a narrow road which soon becomes a mere alleyway, and there to find a small tidal dock and to see a craftsman fitting a new plank to a canal boat in an aroma compounded of fresh-cut timber, hot tar and river mud. It is a scene that for centuries was a commonplace on London River, but which has now become a rarity unbelievably remote from the roaring traffic of the nearby High Street.

The mouth of the River Brent below Thames Lock dries out at low tide, so that at such a time there is a deceptive air of inactivity about the riverside. But Brentford awakens as the blackened, waveless tide creeps back over the mud shoals and lifts against the lower gates of the lock. Incoming and outgoing barges jostle each other in the short tortuous reach of the river up to Brentford Lock, while off the mouth of the Brent the tugs from the Pool manœuvre with a dexterity wonderful to watch as they cast off their tows and pick up others. It was through Brentford that I brought my own boat on to the Thames from the midland canals, dropping down to the head of Thames Lock immediately after the activity of one tide had subsided in order to be the first to lock out on the next. In this way not only is the mêlée of traffic avoided, but a boat bound up river can reap the advantage of the flood tide all the way to Teddington.

Above the mouth of the Brent the scene changes with almost magical swiftness; for the gardens and trees of Kew are on the left, while on the right, so soon as the wharves and cranes of the railway dock are passed, is the park of Syon. In the waste of Greater London and after the bewildering man-made panorama of the lower reaches, Syon Reach is a refreshing contrast. Kew Gardens for all their beauty are self-conscious and never allow the visitor to forget that he is in an urban park. The smaller area of Syon seems more natural and further removed from its surroundings. Cows graze the pasture; wild duck wheel over the watermeadows; herons fly on heavy slow-beating wings or stand stiffly at the river's margin; these things assist the illusion of detachment. It is destroyed by the occasional snort of a loco-motive followed by the clash of buffers, a reminder that workaday Brentford, in the shape of the dockside marshalling yard, lies immediately beyond the high park wall.

Syon was originally a monastery of the Bridgettine Order, founded by Henry V to expiate his father's complicity in the murder of Richard II. The nuns of Syon have a unique record as the only religious community of women which has never been separated since the reign of Mary who temporarily reinstated them at Syon after the dissolution of their house by Henry VIII. On the accession of Elizabeth they were exiled once more and finally settled in Lisbon for over 250 years before returning to Syon Abbey in Devonshire.

The secular history of Syon is bound up with that of the great families of Northumberland and Somerset, and the house and grounds remain substantially as they were when transformed by Robert Adam for Hugh, first Duke of Northumberland, in the years immediately following his succession in 1766. The immense square block with its corner towers and castellated parapet, surmounted now by the great lion which once crowned Northumberland House, is more impressive than beautiful. The same might be said of its interior where comfort, convenience and the precious quality of homeliness have all been sacrificed to a concern for pomp and display which attains a climax in the 'Empire' Anteroom where, after the cold marble magnificence of the Great Hall, the eye is suddenly subjected to an almost overwhelming surfeit of colour, gilding, verd-antique and scagliola work. By far the happiest of these great apartments is the Gallery. It is 136 feet long and only 14 feet wide yet, despite these extraordinary proportions, it is a room of great beauty, an achievement which constitutes a superb tribute to the genius of Robert Adam.

The dining-room of Syon is situated between the Anteroom on the one hand and the Red Drawing-Room on the other, these apartments in turn leading to the Great Hall and the Gallery respectively. The most careful scrutiny did not reveal to me any other means of access to the dining-room either overt or concealed. How were meals served? It seemed incredible that the dishes should be carried from some remote kitchen either through the Great Hall or through the Drawing-Room, but the attendant on duty in the dining-room could shed no light on this little mystery.

The end of Syon Park is marked by a pleasant little boat-house designed by James Wyatt for Hugh, second Duke of Northumberland, and beyond it is Isleworth's quiet waterfront. A fire has left the church, which has been attributed to Wren, a mere shell, but spared the nearby 'London Apprentice' which is one of the most attractive of all Thames-side inns. Moreover, unlike too many hotels on the river which have exploited their attractive sites or architecture and become self-conscious or bogus, the Georgian 'London Apprentice' is an honest house inside as well as out. Long may it remain so. Crowds may throng the towpath along the Kew bank and traffic may roar down the old Bath Road not half a mile away, but the old houses of Isleworth seem to drowse in the security of their calm backwater between the park wall of Syon and the willows of Isleworth Ait. "Watch and Pray", says the sundial on the south wall of the church, "Time passeth away like a shadow".

From the head of Isleworth Ait it is but a short distance to Richmond Lock, the last on the river and the only one under the jurisdiction of the Port of London Authority. It is half-tidal, that is to say craft only make use of the lock between half ebb and half flood. So soon as the water reaches the half-tide mark, the patent sluices of the weir are drawn up so that boats can pass freely on the level. We had timed our departure from Brentford so as to avoid using Richmond Lock, and as we approached the weir footbridge we could see that the warning disc signals which indicate when the sluices are down had been removed.

Richmond Lock and weir is the relatively modern embodiment of proposals repeatedly advanced for many years but never acted upon because they proved highly contentious. In the course of his report to the Common Council of the Corporation of London on the state of the Thames dated December 1770, James Brindley advocates a similar lock and weir between Kew and Mortlake and makes clear the reasons for his proposal:—

"Upon examining that part of the river between Mortlake and Richmond Gardens, I find much time is lost, particularly in neap tides, owing to the shoals and sand-banks arising on or towards the towing-side between these two places, which cannot be passed over for a great part of the tide of ebb, so that vessels not being able to reach this place before high water must remain till the next tide; which they need not do, as the towing path begins at Mortlake, could they have a sufficient depth of water to float them up. To remedy this inconvenience, I would propose a dam to be made across the river, somewhere between Mortlake and Kew Bridge, with a lock at each end. This would receive all vessels from London that could save their tide to this place, and by being come to the towing path would proceed up to the canal* or towards Kingston without hindrance or delay.

"Also all vessels coming down would, for the whole tide, have deep water and an easy passage into the tideway. This would also be very useful in another respect, as it would make Kew Bridge a convenient landing-place for all passengers. and would preserve a pool of water large enough to receive commodiously all vessels which must wait during the flood-tide before they can proceed towards London. The river being thus sufficiently raised, will render the navigation to the mouth of the canal and towards Kingston extremely easy, and be of great utility to the several towns of Brentford, Isleworth, Richmond and Twickenham, and render that part of the country in general perhaps the most delightful spot in Europe.

"The expense of this dam and two locks (from the best accounts I have been able to get of the price of materials) will be about £17,500."

Brindley's arguments seem unassailable, but in fact both this and similar proposals made during the nineteenth century were vigorously and successfully opposed on the grounds that the penning up of so much tidal water would cause silting in London River by reducing the scour of the ebb and would also hamper shipping moving seaward on the ebb. Thus it was not until 1890 that the Bill authorising the construction of Richmond Lock was passed, the lock being opened by the Duke of York on May 19th 1894. The decline of commercial traffic may have reduced its

* Brindley favoured canal as opposed to river navigation, but the scheme for a canal from Isleworth to the Oxford Canal at Hampton Gay was dropped when the Grand Junction Canal was authorised.

13   A Boatbuilding Yard and Workshops at Battersea

From a watercolour by Samuel Scott, circa 1760

In the collection of William Hartmann, Esq.

utility but, as Brindley forecast, it has vastly improved the appearance and amenities of the Thames at Richmond.

Above Richmond Lock, three bridges span the river in quick succession; first Twickenham Bridge opened in 1933 and, with the exception of the new Waterloo Bridge, the latest to be built over the Thames; next the ugly iron railway bridge, and lastly the lovely balustraded Richmond Bridge (Figure 14), built by Tontine as a toll bridge in 1777 to the designs of James Paine.

Until Henry VII, Earl of Richmond in Yorkshire, rechristened it with his own title, Richmond was known as Sheen, and as such played no small part in the mediæval history of England. The old name which, since Saxon days, has signified brightness or splendour, must have been apt, for the Palace of Sheen was a popular Royal resort and was enriched, enlarged or rebuilt successively by the Houses of Lancaster, Plantagenet and Tudor. Damaged in the Civil War and finally demolished during the reign of Queen Anne, only a gateway and a few fragments of the original palace remain, though the name is perpetuated by a group of buildings near the bridge which is known as the "Old Palace". Fortunately, however, the popularity of Richmond Park with the House of Hanover did much to recompense the town architecturally for the loss of its ancient splendour. The proximity of the Lodge in the Old Deer Park made Richmond the resort of a fashion which enriched its Green and its Hill with the Georgian graces of Maids of Honour Row, Old Palace Terrace and Trumpeting House; of Doughty House and the Wick. Though Richmond has virtually become a part of Greater London and its streets are congested with traffic, these and other lesser memorials of the age of elegance still affirm its individual and historic character. Moreover, although the great block of the Star & Garter Home has replaced the famous hotel of that name on the crown of Richmond Hill, the celebrated view of the river from that hill has not yet been badly marred. The grounds of Ham House, once the home of the Earls of Dysart, on the south bank, and the parks of Marble Hill and Orleans House on the north, have happily checked riverside 'development'.

Once fashionable Twickenham, whose waterfront begins by Eel Pie island, has not been so fortunate. Seen from the river there is little to remind the traveller that here dwelt Pope, Swift, Fielding, Gay, Cibber, Kneller, Sir William Chambers and Lady Mary Wortley Montague. The King of eighteenth-century Twickenham was, of course, Horace Walpole, but his fantastic Gothic 'Palace' of Strawberry Hill is almost hidden behind bungalows, while gravel workings have devastated the riverside lands on the Surrey side.

Almost directly opposite Strawberry Hill, a small obelisk indicates the limit of jurisdiction of the Port of London Authority, and it is the Thames Conservancy which controls the great weir and locks of Teddington, which lie just round the bend of the river.

All the way from Brentford we had been following a tug with a train of loaded lighters bound for Kingston Gasworks and, not knowing the capacity of the locks at

21

Teddington, we wrongly supposed that we should have to wait until they had locked through. Not only are there three locks, but the chamber of the largest of them received the tug, its train and our own 70-feet boat with room to spare. Rebuilt in 1931, it is 650 feet long by 25 feet wide and can, I believe, claim to be the longest lock in the British Isles excluding, possibly, certain dock entrance locks. The locks on the Manchester Ship Canal, for example, though of much greater width are 50 feet shorter.

Throughout the eighteenth century shallows in the river at Teddington were a great hindrance to navigation, and it was not until June 20th 1811 that the first lock was opened for traffic. Built by the Corporation of the City of London, who were at that time responsible for river maintenance as far as Staines, it was situated on the Middlesex side and was 120 feet long by 20 feet wide with a pair of intermediate gates for use by small craft. In 1858 the small middle lock was opened to cater for the growing volume of pleasure traffic.

A certain Richard Savory of Strand-on-the-Green was the first lock-keeper at Teddington, to be succeeded by his son and grandson. Three times in eleven years he was robbed of the toll takings, on the first occasion with violence. Considering the isolated situation of many Thames lock cottages, such cases are rare in the history of the river, so that it is strange that on this most frequented reach the unfortunate Savory should have been repeatedly singled out for attack. After the third assault his son, Richard Savory II, not unnaturally appealed to the Corporation for: "Sufficient fire Arms in case of attack on Lock as follows: A Blunderbuss and a bayonet; of course a double Arms in case of misfire, a brace of Pistols and ammunition also a horn for Powder". The Corporation granted him "a blunderbuss with a bayonet attached thereto".*

Today, lock-keepers seeking promotion move progressively down the river because, owing to the greater density of traffic on the lower reaches, the rate of pay increases proportionately. It is a beneficent custom of the Conservancy to reward lock-keepers of long service and good record by posting them at Teddington shortly before they are due to retire. This means that they enjoy the maximum rate of pension on retirement. In addition, assistant lock-keepers are always on duty to deal with the work involved at this busy station, which includes the regulation of the famous weir.

The first broad tideless reach of Thames between Teddington and Kingston is not particularly distinguished. The ubiquitous riverside bungalow makes its appearance now that regulated waters favour riverside lawns, while the river approach to Kingston and the once pleasant Canbury Gardens is now dominated by the new power station. The present fine stone bridge at Kingston, built in 1828 and widened in 1914, stands a little above the site of the old wooden bridge which features in Figure 16. It was from the latter that, by order of the local court, the hostess of the King's Head Inn was ducked for scolding before a large crowd in April 1745. This

* F. S. Thacker, *The Thames Highway*.

22

was one of the last recorded cases of the infliction of this rough and ready, but possibly effective, punishment.

Bungalows and riverside houses have monopolised the banks of the river to such an extent that there is a great lack of convenient temporary moorings on the lower reaches of the Thames, particularly for large craft. A pleasant exception is the public wharf of Kingston, which is situated just above the bridge on the Hampton Wick side and adjoining the tree-lined edge of Hampton Court Park. Its only disadvantage is that an east wind wafts across the water the smell of Kingston's peculiarly odoriferous tannery. It was here that we made our first stop after entering the Thames at Brentford, and how enjoyable it was to sit on deck in the late spring sunshine and watch the varied traffic passing by: rowing boats and racing shells; launches and cabin cruisers of every shape and size; pleasure steamers; steam tugs and lighters and, last and largest, the small Dutch coasters carrying coal from the Tyne to Kingston Gasworks. These last, with masterly skill, navigate Kingston Bridge with what seems only a matter of inches to spare. Why, one is forced to conjecture, should the Dutch have found their way into the time-honoured and purely domestic Tyne coal trade? Is it because we are losing our spirit of initiative and our capacity for hard work? Certainly these Dutch ships, beautifully clean and trim and generally owned and operated by a family who live aboard, have become increasingly common round our coasts since the war. The impudent raid of the Dutch fleet on the Medway in the seventeenth century forced England to face the fact that her much vaunted 'wooden walls' were not as inviolable as she had supposed. Today, the enterprising descendants of these raiders have penetrated much further inland on their lawful and peaceable occasions. Can this mean that the steel walls of our mercantile marine are, metaphorically, rusting away? Perhaps we have not troubled to consider the question.

The name and historical fame of the Royal Borough of Kingston are both linked with the celebrated King stone—the Coronation Stone, it is said, of seven Saxon Kings. This formerly stood in the market place imprisoned and well-nigh overwhelmed by iron railings and conical capped stone pillars of peculiarly hideous aspect. It has now been removed, railings and all, to a less conspicuous position near the ancient mediæval bridge over the Hogsmill Brook. It seems a pity that the railings could not have been conveniently lost in the process of removal.

In face of the outward march of Greater London, Kingston has not maintained its individual and historical character so effectually as Richmond. Its best claim to distinction today is as a shopping centre, and in this context we came to the conclusion during our brief stay that it could have but few rivals among provincial centres in the south of England. There is, for example, an excellent open market, a cake shop which purveys confections of pre-war richness and, dominating all, an enormous department store modelled on transatlantic lines which displays a dazzling wealth and variety of stock combined with a mechanistic efficiency of organisation that a disorderly individual mind finds almost terrifying to contemplate.

It is a relief to turn from the crowds, the escalators and the bright lights to the quiet seclusion of a modest but no less famous business on Kingston's waterfront where, in a craftsmanly and intensely personal atmosphere of order in disorder, some of the finest sails in the world are made.

Adjoining Kingston is Surbiton, a name which automatically suggests all that is derogatory in the word suburbia. 'Sunday morning in Surbiton'—the phrase makes the heart sink; we can hear the radios playing and smell the Sunday joints roasting in street after painfully genteel street of desirable detached residences; we can see the woman in the fur coat taking her tartan-collared Cairn for a purposive airing under the veiled surveillance of innumerable coyly curtained windows. But why should the name Surbiton be singled out for such associations, for in what respect does it differ from any other of London's dormitories? I cannot answer, for I have never visited its streets, but having seen it from the water I would say that it has been maligned. Its riverside walk, bright with beds of flowers, looked pleasant enough, while its riverside houses compare favourably with the bungalows of later date which line other reaches of the Thames—at neighbouring Thames Ditton, for instance, of whose waterfront I carried away an impression only of bungalows and waterworks.

Meanwhile, on the Middlesex side the river has been circling Hampton Court Park until, opposite the confluence of the River Mole, there appears this most notable of English domestic buildings, a great rose-red monument to the vaunting ambition of a Cardinal, the rapacity of a King and the genius of a great architect. It is the largest of our royal palaces, though no reigning monarch since George II has lived in it. When he seized the Palace after Wolsey's downfall, Henry VIII was responsible for considerable alterations and enlargements, but when Sir Christopher Wren was commissioned by William and Mary to rebuild and make good the dilapidations of the seventeenth century, he pulled down considerable portions of the Tudor building, including the Long Gallery. Wren's original scheme, in fact, involved its complete demolition, but it was never carried out owing to the death of his royal patrons. Though further work was done during the reigns of Queen Anne and the first two Georges, the last architect employed being William Kent, it was, perhaps, to the advantage of posterity that the Tudor buildings, including part of Wolsey's original palace, have survived. For whereas there are other monuments of Wren's genius, the architecture and embellishment of the earlier building is of great and almost unique historical interest. Its Italianate terra-cotta busts and medallions survive to show how, even at this date, English taste was groping its way towards that flowering which we call the English Renaissance, and which was to reach its zenith in Wren's magnificent building with its carvings by Grinling Gibbons and Gabriel Cibber, its ironwork by Jean Tijou and its painted ceilings by Verrio and Thornhill.

The gardens of Hampton are similar to the Palace in that they were re-designed by Wren, but retain certain features of the earlier Tudor gardens. In addition to the

14　Richmond by the Bridge

From a watercolour by Thomas Hearne, signed and dated 1790

15　A distant view of Windsor Castle: probably taken from Cranbourn Lodge

From a watercolour by John Glover

celebrated vine and the maze they include part of the 'Cardinal's River', an artificial canal or conduit eleven miles long which was built to convey the waters of the Colne to the grounds and, originally, to supply the Palace. It is not the only ancient artificial tributary of Thames; another called the 'Duke of Northumberland's River' also taps the Colne and joins the Thames at Isleworth. It was built by Henry VII to drive the Syon Abbey mills at Twickenham and Isleworth.

Across the green from the Palace stands an attractive group of old buildings, which include the sixteenth-century Royal Mews, the Mitre Hotel and the Old Court House where lived Sir Christopher Wren for the last fifteen years of his life. He died there in 1723 at the ripe old age of ninety-one.

Just beyond the arches of Lutyens' Hampton Bridge is Molesey Lock, the largest on the river after Teddington. Despite complaints of navigation difficulties hereabouts and the recommendations of John Rennie, it was not until August 1815 that the first Molesey Lock was opened. It was rebuilt in 1906. In 1839 a needlemaker with the delightful name of March Peart was lock-keeper, and F. S. Thacker quotes a letter of his to the Corporation of London which makes entertaining reading. "Snell has again been at his tricks," writes the aggrieved needlemaker. "He came down the River in *Good Intent* lug Sep. 10, 11 a.m. Shell's Steam Boat was in sight after him coming with great speed. Soon as the Lug was in the Lock Snell and another Man jumped out and forced the gates to, and placed themselves upon the gates daring me to touch a paddle. My wife hearing a great noise came out with another Female. With them I prevented Snell shutting out the Steam Boat, (he?) using the foulest language that could be uttered." Evidently captain Snell was a boatman of the old school whose good intentions certainly did not extend to new-fangled steamers. I have often admired the patience with which the lock-keepers of today cope with the blunders of the inexpert crews of hired cruisers, but it is evident that their predecessors had their troubles too, though of a different and more violent order.

A little distance above Molesey Lock is Tagg's Island, now known as Casino Island, a name which is sufficient to describe both the hotel that stands upon it and those who patronise it. The island was recently joined to the mainland by a footbridge, for it is a curious psychological fact that no island hotel on the Thames which has had to depend on a ferry, however efficient the ferry service, has ever prospered.

The old nucleus of Hampton makes a pleasant waterside group whose most notable features are Garrick's villa with its Adam façade, and the delightful little piece of classic nonsense by the water's edge which is known as Garrick's Temple. Garrick intended that this should house Roubiliac's statue of Shakespeare, but the Bard has never visited his select suburban retreat and resides in the British Museum. Hampton once boasted one of the best sailing reaches on the river, but subsequent riverside development, notably the banks and buildings of the Metropolitan Waterworks and the stands of Hurst Park race-course, have spoiled this amenity by breaking the wind. The fine open reach at Bourne End is probably the best on the Thames for this sport today.

There is little to be said about the river from Hampton through Sunbury and Walton Bridge to Shepperton Lock, for such riverside land as is free from water-works has been claimed by riverside builders. The Thames-side bungalow has been the subject of much abuse, and it cannot be said that the river has been improved by its prolific growth. The desire to live or to spend week-ends in peace and quiet by the riverside is a perfectly natural and understandable one in our civilisation. That the desire should defeat itself in a straggling Thames-side township where there is neither peace nor quiet is due to the fact that this country is grossly over-populated. It must also be said that although the Thames bungalow may be jerry built, the majority are well kept and freshly painted, their gardens smooth-lawned and bright with flowers in season. The same cannot be said, unfortunately, for some of the riverside property in this neighbourhood, particularly near Walton Bridge, where there is a huddle of shacks and caravans which are a disgrace to the banks of England's premier river.

Prior to the first world war, Thames-side villa architecture seemed to have developed a style of its own seldom to be seen elsewhere, except perhaps for occasional isolated examples in the suburbs of certain seaside resorts. It is prominent at Pangbourne and elsewhere, and consists of a glorious mixture of mock half-timbering, red brick, elaborate painted barge-boarding and other fretted woodwork, the whole not infrequently crowned by turrets with red-tiled pinnacles like fire extinguishers. To add a last touch of the bizarre to this Edwardian-Tudor-Rococo jamboree, large terra-cotta dragons (or are they griffons?) rear from the roof ridge at the gable ends. Judging from the number of these heraldic monsters (varying in size but identical in form) which menace the Thames traveller, their manufacture must once have been quite a profitable local industry.

We view these architectural oddities with a more tolerant eye today because they remind us of a world which has become as remote as the Middle Ages. That world which we see in faded photographs that depict elegant ladies with leg-o'-mutton sleeves and Merry Widow hats reclining in punts deftly propelled by squires immaculate in boaters and white ducks. They lived in a fools' paradise, the sunset of an Age, did they but know it. Yet how we envy them their days of wine and roses! For them God was permanently resident in the English heaven and the world beneath indissolubly right. . . .

The first lock at Sunbury was built in 1812 on John Rennie's recommendation. It was situated further up the cut than the present lock, which dates from 1856. The reason for this change of site is interesting, and explains why the Thames locks are almost invariably to be found at the downstream ends of lock-cuts. By building them thus, the flush, or 'flash' to use the old term, from the lower paddles tends to scour away the bar of silt which the river, in flood times, would otherwise build across the lower mouths of the cuts. Apparently the building of the original lock temporarily affected access to the Barge Wharf at Sunbury, for local residents complained indignantly to the Corporation when barges moored on their property and

16   Kingston-on-Thames, Surrey, 1818

From a watercolour by George Shepherd

In the Ashmolean Museum, Oxford

proceeded incontinently to discharge their cargoes. F. S. Thacker quotes one of these letters, dated August 1812, which throws further light on the uncompromising character of the Thames Bargemen of those days:

". . . Another Bargeman", writes the aggrieved householder, "fastened the Barge rope to a small punt post—I went out to notice the impropriety of fixing the rope of so large a Barge to so small a post.—He answered that if he chose, he might fix the Rope to the knocker of my Street door. The Language used by the Men was very improper to be within hearing of the Ladies of the House."

The great snake bend in the river by Lower Halliford and Shepperton was described as 'most picturesque' before it became so popular and populous, but its shoals were a great obstacle to heavily-laden barges. As long ago as 1802 a 'by-pass' cut was proposed, but it was not until 1935 that the idea was realised by the present Desborough Channel which was built partly for the benefit of navigation and partly as a flood-relief measure. The western end of the Desborough Channel leads the water traveller into a maze of waterways. On his right is the old river channel; immediately ahead the river is divided by D'Oyley Carte Island (so called because Sir Arthur Sullivan once lived on it), while beyond it stands Shepperton Lock. To the left of the lock-tail stretches the great pool below the relief weir into which fall the River Wey, the artificial channel of the Wey Navigation, and the Thames weir channel that follows the original course of the river. This wide tree-sheltered pool is the most southerly point on the course of the Thames. It is also the most attractive place on the river east of Staines, and here we turned aside from the main navigation channel to moor for the night near the 'Lincoln Arms' and to explore, in a borrowed rowing boat, the numerous channels and backwaters.

Old Weybridge wharf at the mouth of the Wey has become a pleasure-boat yard, but barges still trade up the Wey navigation to Guildford. This navigation has a long history, having been constructed by Sir Richard Weston between 1651–3. In 1760 it was extended from Guildford to Godalming, and for a short period during the canal heyday it linked the Thames with the south coast via the Wey and Arun Canal. A single flood-gate controls the short, narrow and tortuous channel which leads to the first deep Wey lock.

With only brief interruptions, bungalows continue to line the river from Shepperton Lock to Penton Hook and Staines. Only by Chertsey Lock and by James Paine's attractive Chertsey Bridge do they thin out at all. The large but shallow lock at Penton Hook, which cuts off a most acute horseshoe bend, was originally opened in 1815, being the most westerly lock to be built at the instance of the City of London. Above it the river soon becomes literally a 'street paved with water' as Staines is approached.

How evocative smells can be, even bad ones! I had not visited Staines for over ten years, but as we sailed up Staines reach a peculiar and not altogether pleasant odour came down the breeze, which instantly and vividly recalled night journeys down the great road to the west which passes through the town. It is a unique, oppressive, slightly sickly smell which indicates that something which has no right to do so is overheating and may soon burst into flames. So much so that on still summer nights, when the smell hangs heavy in the air, it suggests to the unsuspecting motorist that some electrical component on his car is on the point of combustion. In fact, however, the smell is produced in the manufacture of linoleum. Possibly the reason why the inhabitants seem to be content to live with it is because Staines proudly claims to possess the largest linoleum factory in the world.

Apart from Rennie's fine bridge and a group of old houses about the church, Staines is as useful but as undistinguished as its chief product, while its most conspicuous contribution to the riverfront has been an enormous gasworks, the biggest blot on the Thames between Brentford and Oxford. Rennie's bridge succeeded no less than three eighteenth-century structures, one of stone and two of iron, which collapsed in quick succession. The first of these abortive bridges was, sad to relate, the work of a certain Professor of Architecture to the Royal Academy.

The name of Staines is popularly supposed to derive from the ancient stone which, raised upon a plinth of later date, stands on the Middlesex bank of the river not far from the church (Figure 17). It is believed to date from the thirteenth century and is called variously the London Stone, London Mark Stone or City Stone. What was formerly meadowland has now become a Recreation Ground, and our democratic age has presented the stone with an incongruous neighbour in the shape of a concrete-lined paddling pool.

The London Stone used to mark the upstream limit of the jurisdiction of the Corporation of the City of London. Above it the Thames Commissioners were responsible for the river as far up as Cricklade. In 1857 the Thames Conservancy was incorporated and took over the control of what was then called the Lower River Navigation from Staines to Yantlet, their eastern boundary only moving to Teddington when the Port of London Authority was constituted in 1909. When, in 1866, the Conservancy also took over the duties of the Upper Thames Navigation Commissioners, one function of the old Mark Stone disappeared. Yet it remains an important boundary mark. Not only does it stand on the borders of Middlesex, Buckinghamshire and Surrey, but it marks the upstream limit of free fishing. Moreover, with the exception of certain Crown rights, the Conservators own the bed and soil of the river on the downstream side, whereas upstream the bed and soil are the property of riparian owners. The interesting point about these differentiations is that they conform with the ancient law governing tidal rivers. It seems almost certain therefore that the site of the London Stone was originally chosen in the thirteenth century as being the tidal limit of the Thames. Before the river became obstructed by weirs and numerous bridges it is highly probable that, even if the tide did not actually flow as far as Staines, it had an appreciable effect there by backing up the water.

Before 1857 the City of London claimed their right of jurisdiction by means of an annual ceremony. The Lord Mayor came up the Thames in his State Barge accompanied by eight Watermen in full livery. Landing at the meadow, a procession was then formed and a health drunk to the toast of 'God preserve the City of London'. Latterly, like so many ancient customs, the ceremony became vulgarised by horseplay which included the custom of 'bumping' the Mayor and Aldermen on the stone.

A short reach leads from the London Stone to Bell Weir Lock, which was opened in 1818, and whose name perpetuates that of its first keeper, Charles Bell. From it the river banks are more or less built up all the way to Old Windsor Lock, with the notable exception of Runnymede, which has been preserved as an open space. Gate piers designed by Sir Edwin Lutyens which flank the Egham–Windsor road bear inscriptions which record the celebrated encounter between King John and the Barons. Some of the architects of our Welfare State now betray a tendency to claim descent from the Runnymede Barons rather than from Karl Marx, whose popularity as a political ancestor seems to be on the wane. This must occasion bewilderment among the inhabitants of the Elysian Fields, to whom some of our statesmen must appear to bear more than a passing resemblance to King John. On Magna Carta island, where the famous charter of English liberty was signed, stands a large house which is, or was until recently, owned by an M.P. The public are not allowed to land, though whether this taboo constitutes an exercise of or an infringement upon the liberty of the individual is a debatable point. It is at Runnymede that the Thames valley first becomes apparent to the upstream traveller in the wooded slopes of Coopers Hill beyond the meadow. Hereabouts, too, Surrey gives place to Berkshire on the south bank. The latter claims by far the greatest length of Thames-side, as the river forms the boundary of the shire as far upstream as St. John's.

A little distance beyond the edge of Runnymede stands one of the oldest and best known of Thames-side inns, 'The Bells of Ouseley'. Though sorely damaged by a bomb during the war it is happily still with us. No authority that I have consulted so much as guesses at the origin of its name, which for beauty rivals that of the 'Rose Revived' at New Bridge. Another name whose origin seems lost to memory is 'Top of Caps' by which the site of Old Windsor Lock was formerly known. The lock and the long narrow cut which leads from it were opened in 1822. The great loop of the river round Ham Fields, which the cut by-passes, has sinister associations. The footpads and highwaymen who once haunted the Bath Road in the neighbourhood of Colnbrook made use of the river at this point to dispose of the corpses of those whom they robbed and murdered. So much so that the reach became known as 'Colnbrook Churchyard'.

After so many miles of built-up banks, it is a joy, soon after leaving Old Windsor cut, to be able to gaze uninterruptedly across the spacious green vistas of Windsor Home Park to where the great central keep of the castle soars above the distant treetops. Fortunate indeed are the tenants of the Georgian houses which flank the riverside green at Datchet to have such a fair prospect before them. From 1706 until 1851 Datchet possessed a bridge (Figure 18), the only case on the Thames where a long established crossing has disappeared. It was superseded by the present Victoria and Albert bridges at the extremities of the Home Park. The last Datchet bridge must have been the most curious ever to span the river. For as a result of a disagreement, the two county authorities responsible for its construction refused to co-operate with each other in any way. Two hostile construction camps set to work, one using timber as a building medium and the other iron. By what diplomacy and ingenuity the disparate halves were ever satisfactorily united is not recorded.

Romney Lock, originally built in 1793, is a notable exception to the rule, mentioned in connection with Sunbury Lock, that locks should be placed as close as possible to the downstream end of lock cuts. The lock is several hundred yards above the point anciently known as the Eedles, where cut and river join, and where, beneath the nearby railway bridge, we found the stream running more strongly than at any other point on the whole river. Perhaps it was not without significance that when we passed a dredger was at work near the mouth of the cut.

We were naturally anxious to moor at Windsor, but found that this was not easy. What was once the public wharf is monopolised by steamers during the season, and the only alternative is to moor beside the 'Cobbler'. The 'Cobbler' is the upstream end of the long narrow Romney Island formed by the lock-cut. Proposals to connect this end of the island with Windsor by a footbridge have never materialised, so that, without a dinghy, the mooring is inconvenient, involving a long walk round by the lock. As a special concession we were allowed to moor just above the lock and not many yards from the point where, in 1828, the artist must have sat when he drew the picture which appears as a frontispiece to this book (Figure 1). Unlike the plates so far mentioned, the scene he depicted has not since been marred.

St. John's Lock, Lechlade, Gloucestershire

From a drawing by Irene Hawkins

30

17   The Church and City Stone, Staines, Middlesex

From an aquatint by Robert Havell, 1811

Chapter Three

WINDSOR TO SONNING

THE timing of our visit to Windsor could not have been more fortunate. Not only did it coincide with a spell of brilliant weather but with the annual Horse Show, held in the Home Park, not five minutes' walk away from our moorings. No more perfect setting for a show could be imagined than the level turf and tall trees of the park in the fresh untarnished green of mid-May with the great castle upon its hill for background. This long irregular skyline of roof and tower and turret, which has been the fortress of the English kings since the Conqueror, has been so often celebrated in painting, drawing and photograph that it could be called England's Trade Mark (Figure 19). It conveyed the same impression to me as did the Tower of London, and for the same reason. So accustomed are we to ruined castles, that when the eye sees so huge a structure in perfect—almost too perfect—preservation, reason is reluctant to accept its witness. When, against this background, the Household Cavalry in their glittering uniforms performed their musical ride in the show ring, the whole scene seemed too good to be true. Surely those so solid-seeming walls must really be the painted plywood props of pageantry?

Not until one has made a dutiful pilgrimage to the Castle does its solidity become assured. We filed round the splendid but sunless State Apartments (how wise of the Royal Family to pick the south side of the Inner Ward for their private quarters!) and clambered breathlessly to the parapet of the great Keep. The prospect of the Thames valley (Figures 15, 20) from this lofty vantage is renowned. It is still fair, for it reminds us that, despite the heavy depredations of recent years, our country, even in this thickly-populated area, is still richly blessed with trees. Except when some high place endows us with a bird's vision we seldom realise how much we owe to them. Here, in this wide perspective, they still cloak the scars of urban development. The only dominant man-made landmarks which they can neither hide nor flatter here are the naked cooling towers of a distant power station and the crass, uncompromising hulk of the gasometer at Staines.

The jewel of Windsor is the chapel of St. George. The quality of the interior of this most superb example of the Perpendicular style is indeed jewel-like. For the freedom from considerations of thrust and stress conferred upon him by the massive exterior buttresses has enabled the stone-mason to handle his material like a craftsman working in ivory or precious metal, with no thought but to express the beauty of stone in each slender, aspiring shaft and rib. The monuments of each great architectural style bear witness to the high endeavour of generations of craftsmen working within certain conventions, but each striving to excel their predecessors by transcending the limitations imposed by the functional quality of their materials; limitations which originally determined the conventions of the style. As a patient Chinese craftsman converts a solid ivory sphere into a carving of the fragility of a soap bubble, so successive generations pare away the solid substance of an architectural style until, in its ultimate refinement, beauty is all and function almost forgotten in the sheer delight of the craftsman's triumph over the limitations of his material. From such supernatural refinement there can be no advance and no return. Thus the Perpendicular style is the symbol of mediæval twilight; thus the brothers Adam celebrated the obsequies of the English Renaissance. It could therefore be argued that St. George's chapel is decadent by comparison with the great nave vaults of Henry Yevele, where beauty and function remain superbly matched. Yet no building could more appropriately enshrine the memorials of the Age of Chivalry, the stalls of the Garter Knights, their helms and banners.

The College (where war damage is being made good in most exemplary fashion) overwhelms Eton (Figure 1) even as the Castle overshadows Windsor. Consequently, the visitor is apt to overlook minor features of interest which might otherwise claim his attention. Eton's old High Street, for example, where such choice and rare details as a Victorian pillar-box with slender, fluted waist and vertical slot, emphasise a dignified and conservative atmosphere, aloof from hurrying time and traffic; Wren's little architectural joke in Windsor's Town Hall, where the columns within the arcades, inserted to placate Mayoral doubts as to the stability of the building, fail to reach the roof by the space of an inch; the Victorian four-wheelers with their elderly jehus waiting patiently in steep Castle Street to take us for a tour of the Great Park, where cars are taboo; even such curious little oddities as the illuminated clock set in the pavement outside a watchmaker's shop. Then there are the two railway stations. Obviously the Great Western and London South Western Companies spared no expense to pay due homage to Royalty, for surely never were two relatively unimportant branch lines equipped with such grandiose termini.

We sailed away from Windsor after two days intensive exploration, having arranged to meet friends at Maidenhead and allowing, as we thought, ample time for the short journey. But we had not reckoned with Boveney Lock on a Saturday afternoon. Here we experienced our only serious delay and our only anxious moments in the whole of our journey up the river. We arrived to find the short tail-cut below the lock completely filled with 'wet bobs', some in fours and pairs, but the majority in single skiffs. Three quarters of an hour passed before we were able to enter the lock, and during the whole of this time we must needs keep manœuvring our heavy craft to counter the wind and the back eddy from the weir which would otherwise have swung her round to crush several of the fragile skiffs which thronged

18   Datchet Ferry, near Windsor, Berkshire

From an aquatint by Robert Havell, 1811

about us with complete disregard for our difficulties or their own safety. When we finally entered the lock, a further long delay ensued while the skiffs were packed into the chamber behind us like sardines into a can. We came to the conclusion that the lock-keeper at Boveney had the most thankless job on the river, and wondered why the Conservancy and the College authorities did not insist that the boys make fuller use of the rollers which are provided for small craft.

Midway between Boveney Lock and the acute bend known as Ruddle's Pool is the upper parting of the Clewer stream which makes an island of Windsor race-course. In 1792 the Thames Commissioners proposed making this stream the navigable channel and building a lock on it, but the scheme was dropped and the present lock built in 1838.

The curious name of Monkey Island, a short distance below Bray Lock, is popularly supposed to have been derived from the monkeys on the painted ceiling of a little fishing lodge, built on the island by the second Duke of Marlborough. Thacker, however, stoutly refuted this and maintained the theory that the island was originally called Monk Eye or Eyot, a name recalling monastic fishing rights. If he was right, then most probably the corrupted name was responsible for Marlborough's monkeys, and not vice versa.

It is interesting to record that the shallow lock at Bray was originally used only in times of low water; otherwise all four gates were opened and traffic passed straight through without payment of toll. It is described as being 'without sides', so presumably, instead of a masonry chamber, it had sloping grass sides such as may still be seen at some of the old locks on the Kennet or the Wey. Bray village, cure of the immortal turncoat Vicar, is described by a by-gone guidebook writer as "one of the quaintest and most picturesque in England" being, he adds, "a week-end retreat . . . sufficiently far from railways to prevent the incursion of trippers". The motor car soon put an end to that by making Bray an adjunct of Maidenhead, its 'quaintness' profitably combined with all the latest 'mod. cons.'. Yet the term 'week-end retreat' suggests that even in the railway age Bray had realised the commercial possibilities of the Picturesque.

The contributions of the railway builders to the Thames scene are generally not distinguished. Though doubtless admirable in engineering principle, the majority of their bridges over the river do not succeed in combining beauty with their utility. In this respect it is a sad fact that the first railway works were also the best. Thus it is that it is not until he approaches Maidenhead that the upstream traveller sees before him a railway bridge that is really worthy of the Thames. When the original main line of the Great Western Railway was surveyed to cross the river at this point, the Thames Commissioners insisted that the towpath and navigation channel must remain entirely unobstructed. To comply with this stipulation the engineer, Isambard Kingdom Brunel, with characteristic daring, designed his magnificent bridge, which possesses the greatest and flattest brick-built spans in the world. Wiseacres confidently predicted that the bridge would collapse beneath the weight of locomotives which we would regard as little more than toys, yet to this day Brunel's bridge stands fast under the thunder of the great West of England expresses. It makes a worthy neighbour for the fine stone bridge which carries the Bath road across the river. Construction of the latter was authorised in 1772, although the old timber bridge which originated in 1297, if not earlier, was still in use as late as 1776. It was maintained by an ancient grant of three trees a year to be cut from the King's Forest in the Royal Manor of Bray.

It is doubtless the proximity of the Bath road and the earliest railway through the Thames valley which made Maidenhead's reputation as the most popular pleasure boating centre on the river. The objective of the vast majority of the hirers of punts, rowing boats and day launches has always been Cliveden Reach, which entails the passage through Boulter's Lock. In the heyday of the river before the first world war it was recorded that as many as 1,000 small craft and 100 launches used the lock on a single summer Sunday. The present lock was originally built in 1828, but to cope with this traffic the Conservancy rebuilt and enlarged it in 1912 to a size comparable with Molesey and only exceeded by Teddington. The popularity of Boulter's has made it the most celebrated lock on the river, and the number of railway compartments displaying photographs of its crowded chamber must once have run into hundreds. Long before the punt and parasol era, however, Boulter's was a station of great importance on the river. There was a flash lock at this point as early as the sixteenth century, whereas, until Romney Lock was built in 1793, the Thames remained completely unobstructed by lock or weir between Boulter's and the sea. For a time, indeed, an Act of 1770 specifically prohibited the construction of any lock or weir between Maidenhead Bridge and the City of London, a fact which accounts for the comparatively recent date of all the lower locks so far mentioned. This same Act of 1770 authorised the construction of eight pound locks between Burcot and Maidenhead of which 'Boltus Lock' was the first to be opened in 1772. It was situated on the opposite side of the river to the present lock, near Taplow Mill.

The famous Cliveden Reach between Boulter's and Cookham Locks has been described by many writers as the most beautiful on the whole course of the river. The broad meadows on the one hand and the steep hanging woods of Cliveden and Hedsor falling sheer to the water's edge on the other, these certainly make a glad sight after so many built-up and scenically undistinguished miles in the lower reaches. Moreover, they were looking their best when we sailed through the reach on a sunny May morning. But I confess I prefer the less celebrated and less sophisticated beauty which is to be found on some of the higher reaches, and in any case there is little that I could profitably add to the eulogies of others. Cliveden Court was designed by Sir Charles Barry for the Duke of Westminster in 1850, and later, after it had passed to the Astor family, it became celebrated in the between-war years as the headquarters of the 'Cliveden Set'. High above the treetops, the great house gazes arrogantly down upon the river. But I thought that however much money I possessed I would prefer to live in the ferryman's cottage at the delightfully named My Lady Ferry. Set beneath the steep woods and facing south, it enjoys a sunny and sheltered situation and yet stands high enough up the steep bank to be out of the reach of floods; a less ostentatious but much pleasanter site for a house.

The lock-keeper at Cookham may also be envied for his lovely lock with its long tree-shaded cut. South of it, two backwaters, one a weir channel, encircle Formosa Island which is claimed to be the largest on the river. But the old main course of the river sweeps round to the north of the lock and formed the navigation channel until the lock and cut were completed in 1830. The Commissioners were compelled to carry out this work because of the rapids and shoals which obstructed the old navigation, and which, despite their repeated appeals, the local landowner, Lord Boston of Hedsor, refused to remedy. They must have felt very aggrieved when, so soon as the lock was opened, that nobleman promptly added insult to injury by claiming for the loss of use of the towing path. After much litigation the wretched Commissioners had to pay him £1,200 in damages and costs, a very substantial sum at that time. Enclosed by weirs at each end, this old Hedsor stream is the only considerable reach on the Thames to which the public have no access.

The curious little Victorian iron bridge at Cookham, near the mouth of the cut, is one of the few bridges on the river where a toll is still charged. Beyond it the riverside bungalows begin again and continue all the way to Bourne End where the fine, open sailing reach begins. Here a strong breeze was whipping up the water into sizeable waves, and the members of the Upper Thames Sailing Club were out in strength to take advantage of such perfect sailing weather. We did our best to give them a wide berth as we forged along to the end of the reach where Quarry Woods slope down to the river on the Berkshire side. Beneath these slopes we saw two objects of interest. One was a lovely little steam launch at Wooton's boathouse, the only example of this once-common Thames craft which we saw on the river; the other was an extraordinary castellated bungalow which looked as if it might well have begun life as a Moroccan fortress at Denham studios. At this point we swung northwards into Marlow Reach and saw directly ahead the gates of Marlow Lock and the spire of the church.

Marlow is a market town of respectable antiquity which was once noted as a centre of the Buckinghamshire lace trade. It boasts a fine broad high street, some gracious specimens of seventeenth-century and Georgian architecture, and a nineteenth-century church whose tall spire is a prominent landmark in this part of the Thames valley. The graceful suspension bridge was erected at the same time as the church. Proximity to Greater London and to the attractions of the Thames has changed the character of Marlow. Typical of this latter day transformation is the 'Compleat Angler' hotel, beautifully situated between bridge and weir on the Berkshire bank. This was formerly the modest 'Angler' Inn and readers may be left to infer the significance of this change of name and status.

It was at Marlow that Shelley spent what was probably the happiest year of his life, walking in the woods and fields of Medmenham or gliding through the Hurley backwaters in his little boat the *Vaga*. The Thames is associated with the lives of so many famous men that to mention all of them in a book about the river would be to write a mere catalogue of worthies. But Shelley deserves a special mention, for no one knew or loved the river better. Though he could not be described as a 'water poet', Shelley's life story reveals the great attraction which water always held for him. It was strange yet fitting that this element which he loved should ultimately be the cause of his early death.

As we found at other Thames-side towns, the lack of facilities for visitors arriving by water at Marlow is remarkable. We could discover no reasonable moorings whatever, and were eventually forced to lie beside the towpath beyond Court Gardens in water so shallow that we could not approach the bank. In view of their potential contribution to revenue during the season, this discouragement of river visitors seems strange.

In Edwardian days, when the internal-combustion engine began to oust the Victorian steam launch, the new power resulted in the evolution of a new design of launch which soon became as characteristic of the Thames as the curious architecture to which I have already referred. A shapely white hull bore an ornate but beautifully built cabin of varnished mahogany which was mounted right aft, there being a spacious open cockpit forward whose occupants were protected from the elements by a permanent awning. Polished brass fittings and a traditional 'Surrey fringe' round the awning put the finishing touches to this elegant contemporary of the Edwardian motor carriage. Fashions change on the river more slowly than they do on the road, but change they do none the less. Examples of this traditional type of Thames day-launch are now becoming rarer each year, and soon it seems destined to follow the steam launch into limbo. In its place have come large numbers of low slipper-stern launches which are literally aquatic motor cars and which produce a wash more damaging than that set up by craft many times their size. At Marlow, just as dusk was falling over the river, one of these slipper-stern boats of unprecedented size and chromium-plated vulgarity came tearing downstream to leave a wash like a miniature Severn bore which lapped the towpath and set our ponderous craft rocking like a punt. Such ill-mannered water-motorists are unfortunately becoming all too common on the lower reaches of the Thames.

A little distance up Marlow Reach stands Bisham Abbey, close to the river but part screened from it by trees. It was originally a preceptory of the Knights Templar, an association which has been perpetuated in the name of nearby Temple Lock. It then became an Abbey whose great church housed, among other illustrious dead, the body of the great Nevill, Earl of Warwick, who was slain amid the bloody wreckage of his fortunes on Barnet Heath. At the dissolution, Henry VIII presented the property to his poor discarded wife, Anne of Cleves. The Abbey, like so many others, was completely destroyed and only a portion of the domestic buildings survives in the present house. From Anne, the house passed to the Hoby family, one

19 Windsor Castle
and the Thames at
Windsor, Berkshire

From a print of 1865

20 Windsor Castle
from Cooper's Hill
in 1798

*From a drawing by J.
Farington, R.A., en-
graved by J. C. Stadler*

View of WINDSOR CASTLE from Coopers-hill.

of whom, Sir Thomas Hoby, was charged by Queen Mary with the custody of Princess Elizabeth. In the little church of Bisham, which stands on the very brink of the Thames, this same Sir Thomas rests with his half-brother beneath a great memorial erected by his widow, Lady Elizabeth Hoby. Its long and glowing epitaph ends with the admonitory words:

> 'Thus live they dead, and we lerne wel therby,
> That ye, and we, and all the world must dye.'

It is the ghost of the Lady Elizabeth that is said to haunt Bisham, eternally lamenting her alleged crime of beating her small son to death for blotting his copy-books, and eternally, like Lady Macbeth, trying to cleanse her crime-stained hands. It is said that her ghost appears in negative, that is to say with white dress and black face and hands. This curious detail seems to give the superstition more substance, because it appears so unlikely that anyone should invent or imagine such a strange transfiguration.

In the eighteenth century, Bisham became the property of the Vansittart–Neale family, who held it until very recently. But in the latest chapter of its long history the ancient house has suffered a second dissolution. The heir of the family was killed in the second world war, and Bisham has now become a 'National Physical Recreation Centre'. Despite a larger staff than the family were able to command, the place looks unkempt and forlorn. Might it be suggested that the most urgent as well as the most practical and satisfying form of Physical Recreation which this democratic body could indulge in would be to set to work to put its house in the order worthy of its history?

A very short but attractive reach leads from Temple to Hurley Lock. The banks are wooded, and the Hurley backwater reveals a view of the beautifully situated Georgian manor house of Harleyford. Both Temple and Hurley Locks were originally built after the Act of 1770 which I referred to in connection with Boulter's. F. S. Thacker, writing in 1920, records the unique preservation at Hurley of the old wooden winch which was used to draw the barges through the original flash lock. It stood on the Buckinghamshire bank just above the present weir.

Hurley village has gone the way of Bray, and if any of its erstwhile villagers could return, the interior of their village pub would astonish them. Hurley reach is reminiscent of Cliveden, for here there is the same contrast between steep slopes on the one hand and level meadows on the other. Two large modern houses crown these slopes, one neo-Georgian, the other architecturally unclassifiable, their terraced gardens falling towards the water. But they are not so favoured as Cliveden, for an appalling collection of caravans and shacks have multiplied like mushrooms in the meadows opposite.

At the head of Hurley reach the navigation makes a sudden turn out of the wide river into a narrow channel between the north bank and an island called Frogmill Ait. The turning is not only acute but blind owing to the trees which cover both the bank and the island. An old friend, with an intimate knowledge of the river, whom we had met at Staines had warned us to proceed with caution at this point. Though I recognised it at once from his description I had been unable to pin-point it on my map at the time because he had called it, not Frogmill, but 'the Poison Ducks'. "That's what we call it", he had said, and could give no explanation of this most curious name. I had come to the conclusion that it must perpetuate some hoary Thames joke or some historic act of sabotage inspired by a rural vendetta. In fact, as I subsequently discovered, its origin is far more ancient, coming straight and but slightly corrupted from the Norman–French of the Middle Ages. It records the fact that there was an ancient fish weir or duct at this place, set up, most probably, by the Abbey of Medmenham. Centuries shrank at the thought that our friend had unwittingly used a term which the river folk first heard on the lips of a Cistercian monk from Normandy within a hundred years of the Conquest, and which they crudely anglicised. Even so did our soldiers massacre French words and phrases in the first world war. Thacker records another 'Poison Ducks' near Boveney, but this is not situated on the navigation channel and may have vanished from local use or memory.

The Cistercian community at Medmenham had shrunk to two when the Abbey was dissolved. Thereafter it lay wholly or partially ruined until the eighteenth century when it was ingeniously restored by Italian workmen to the orders of Sir Francis ('Hell Fire') Dashwood, the eccentric and notorious squire of West Wycombe. It then became the scene of the orgies and sacrilegious ceremonies of the 'Knights of St. Francis of Wycombe'. There can be little doubt that countrymen and river men alike gave Medmenham a wide berth in those days and that awed whispers of lewd or impious doings too terrible to name passed from ear to inquisitive ear. It was even said that the workmen who rebuilt the house had been supernaturally spirited away when their task was done. Nor can there be any doubt that Sir Francis enjoyed it all hugely. It is difficult for us to regard the orgies of the Knights of St. Francis quite so seriously, for were they any more than a sophisticated version of the schoolboy game of 'dares'? As for the mock-religious ceremonies, assuming they ever took place, they necessarily imply a confirmed and orthodox religious belief and not the lack of it. The truly irreligious could experience no wicked thrills in the celebration of liturgical parodies. The old grey walls of Medmenham have outlived the sacred and the profane, and the antics of Sir Francis have not endowed them with any sinister quality. Hung with wistaria and surrounded by smooth lawns, they looked very peaceful and very lovely in the sunlight as we passed by.

It is between Medmenham and Hambleden that the upstream traveller first experiences truly open country. The river banks are 'undeveloped' and the wide fields lead the undistracted eye away to the distant uplands of the Chiltern chalk, their generous contours maned with beech woods. This new spaciousness conferred a sense of freedom and we felt we had left behind the last vestiges of London's

21   The Thames near Fawley Court, Henley, Oxfordshire

From an aquatint by Robert Havell, 1811

influence as we sailed past Georgian Culham Court, set high in its sloping parkland, and so came to Hambleden Lock.

Hambleden, with its fine white weather-boarded mill and spectacular weir, is usually a quiet and pleasant place, but at the time of our passing extensive repairs to the weir were in progress and its calm was disturbed by the clatter of pile-drivers. The lock was first opened in 1773, and one of its early keepers was Caleb Gould, a name common to several men who served the river here and at Hurley. He died at the great age of ninety-two, and his tombstone can be seen in the churchyard of the little hamlet of Remenham. It bears Gay's disillusioned lines for epitaph:—

> 'This world's a jést,
> And all things show it;
> I thought so once,
> But now I know it.'

Did the old man choose the lines himself? One would have thought that a lifetime spent on the river would have induced a less cynical philosophy, but perhaps importunate bargemen wore him down.

From Hambleden Lock the river sweeps round to the southwards, and we were soon passing Temple Island to enter what is probably the best known stretch of water in the world—the famous Henley 'straight mile'. The little Classic 'temple', which gives the island its name and is of too recent a date to feature in Figure 21, looked sadly forlorn and dilapidated. It is to be hoped that someone will take it in hand before it is too late, for it is not only a charming little 'whimsy' but a notable landmark from its situation at the starting point of the Regatta course. Although it was still only the month of May, we found that the piles and floating booms which mark this course were already being set down. Midway along the Henley Mile the north bank passes from Buckinghamshire into Oxfordshire.

As we approached Henley town we anticipated the same mooring difficulty which we had experienced elsewhere, but in this case we were pleased to find that we were wrong. An enterprising and thoughtful Town Council has provided excellent mooring facilities for visiting craft beside their pleasant public gardens. These include convenient mooring rings and access to a drinking-water tap. It was a novel experience for us to be issued by an attendant with a 'Mooring Ticket' for all the world as though we had parked a car, but no reasonable boat-owner could object to the modest fee demanded for this all too rare amenity. Other Thames-side towns might take note of the fact that as a result of this public hospitality we extended our stay at Henley from one night to ten, during which time we fully replenished our depleted stores of food and fuel besides patronising the town's hotels and its small theatre. In fact, the provision of mooring facilities should be regarded, not as a grudged concession to non-ratepayers, but as a cheap and profitable investment.

In the neighbourhood of its railway station Henley exhibits architecture reminiscent of a seaside resort of the ugliest type, but with this exception the essential character of the old town is surprisingly little changed. The view as we looked back from our moorings was in no respect radically dissimilar from that depicted in Figure 22. Moreover, while it is true that there are plenty of hotels, teashops and purveyors of antiques to beguile the visitor, Henley has not, despite the fame of its Regatta, prostituted itself to that opulent but unprepossessing element which is to be found disporting itself elsewhere in the Thames valley with the airs but not the graces of nobility. To give only one instance, there is the old 'Angel', which stands by Henley Bridge exactly as it did long years before George Shepherd depicted it in 1818. Enjoying such an unrivalled site on the very brink of the river, how easily might its interior have become the equivalent of the flashier type of West-End bar with prices to match. The clientele which is attracted by this sort of spurious glitter is notoriously fickle, and the proprietor who seeks to capture such trade at the expense of local custom wakes up one day to find that his birds have flown to new allurements. The 'Angel' has wisely avoided such pitfalls. It purveys food and drink at honest prices, does not regard the beer drinker as beneath contempt and, most significant of all, it has not frightened local people out of its bar. It was pleasant to look down from the bow windows of this hospitable inn upon the traffic of the river and on the fine eighteenth-century bridge with its sculptured keystones of Isis and Thamesis. These heads, the work of Horace Walpole's friend Mrs. Damer, look immensely effective at night when they are thrown into sharp relief by the lights which indicate the main arch. I shall always remember, too, standing on our deck at midnight in the light of a setting moon and listening to a chorus of nightingales singing in the hanging woods of Park Place. Henley was our first port of call on the river which we left with a genuine sense of regret.

Marsh Lock, at the head of Henley reach, is another of the 1770 series. It is attractively situated, but its approaches are awkward from the navigational point of view, particularly if there is a strong stream running, because they are exposed to the currents of the weir channel. For this reason proposals were made to transfer the lock to a better site on the Oxfordshire bank but were never carried out. Moored above this lock we were astonished to see what appeared to be a genuine Venetian Gondola. Had that strange black shape come stealing down the river with lantern agleam that night when we lay at Henley, we should have fancied ourselves bewitched by the magic of the moon and the nightingales.

At Poplar Eyot, past the mouth of the long tree-shadowed Hemmerton back-water, riverside 'ribbon development' begins again with a vengeance and continues, on one bank or the other, all the way to Shiplake Lock. At Lower Shiplake, which is some distance by water from the lock, there are to be seen some unusually elaborate examples of twentieth-century Elizabethan. Just below Shiplake Lock the tributary Loddon, lonely Loddon as it is often called, completes its course from the heathlands of Stratfield Saye. It possesses another outlet to the Thames above the lock via the backwater called St. Patrick's stream. Moreover, it is almost certain that the head of this backwater formed yet a third mouth of the Loddon until

Shiplake weir was raised, when the direction of its flow was reversed and it became an outfall.

On emerging from Shiplake Lock a notice-board warns the navigator to hug the Oxfordshire bank to avoid the draw from the weir. Fortunately, we did not take this instruction too literally, for the wash of our passing momentarily uncovered the ugly head of an old pile some distance from the bank. Could it have been a forgotten relic of the old weir?

The river presently veers away from the high ground of Shiplake to wind through a somewhat desolate region of level flood-meadows and islands overgrown with willow and alder, which makes the traveller welcome the sight of the seventeenth-century brick bridge and the sheltering trees of Sonning. Sonning village has virtually become an exclusive dormitory of Reading. Much as some of us may regret the tendency of expanding towns to draw surrounding villages within their orbit, at Sonning, as in other similar cases, it has at least favoured the survival of the substance, if not the spirit. If some of the old houses in Sonning have been restored to a charm that is almost too self-conscious and sophisticated, that is surely preferable to dilapidation leading ultimately to condemnation. In its tree-sheltered hollow by the river, Sonning basks in the sun, roses rioting over old walls of brick or colour wash. Like the face of an actress, we know that its beauty is not wholly natural, yet we cannot resist its attraction.

Sonning was once of ecclesiastical importance as the centre of the Saxon see of Wessex, and until the sixteenth century the Bishops of Salisbury retained a Palace here. No trace remains, but a house called 'The Deanery', designed by Sir Edwin Lutyens, enjoys the old walled gardens of its predecessor. Sonning is exceptional, too, in that its parish boundary extends to both banks of the river. Owing to the half-hour's extension of licensing hours enjoyed by Oxfordshire, a procession of thirsty folk from the 'White Hart' or the 'Bull' on the Berkshire side may be seen hurrying over the bridge soon after ten o'clock to obtain 'one for the road' at the 'French Horn'.

Unlike so many of the mills on the river which are either disused or have vanished altogether, Sonning Mill is still very much alive. Here, occasionally, there comes a tug with a lighter load of grain from the Port of London, the last survival of the traditional commercial traffic of the Thames west of Staines. For centuries the Thames continued to be a great commercial highway despite a host of difficulties: shoals and shallows; the obstructions of land and mill owners; dangerous and often ruinous Flash weirs or pound locks; innumerable tolls, sometimes prohibitive: bridge tolls, lock tolls, tolls for the use of the towpath, tolls for ferrying men or horses across the river wherever the towpath changed from bank to bank; disputes with farmers who claimed monopolies of horse haulage over certain reaches; trouble with the rough gangs of bow-hauliers or 'scuffle-hunters'* as they were known on the river. One by one all these natural and man-made hazards have been

* The name was also applied to the cargo thieves in the Port of London.

removed until today there is no finer or better maintained river navigation in England than the Thames, while mechanical power has made the difficulties of towpath towing a thing of the past. Is it not ironical, therefore, that trade on the river beyond Staines should now be almost non-existent? The last considerable trader on the Upper Thames was the redoubtable Emmanuel Smith, whose name is still well remembered.

Sonning Lock, highest of the 1770 series, once had a keeper of remarkable character in the person of Michael Sadler. He was appointed to the lock in 1845 and served it for forty years. A great bee-keeper and inventor of the Berkshire type of hive, such time as he had to spare from his lock and his bees, he spent in writing verse. Thacker's quotation from his major work, a learned and highly moral discourse on the art of the apiarist, is worth repeating. Consciously or unconsciously the author gave it the delightfully onomatopœic title of 'Special Pleas for Honey Bees':—

'They nothing care for vaulted dome, but keep it cool and give them room.
Though to the south their house be made, by all means keep it in the shade;
For when the weather cold becomes, they cluster well beneath the combs;
But if they get intensely warm, nothing is left them but to swarm . . .
I think enough is said to show bees are the pets you ought to know.
They give you pleasure, bring you gain; with but the smallest risk of pain.
Long has it proverbial been that industry in bees is seen;
This lesson then for me and you: work while there is work to do.'

His lines on Sonning are less happy though they do at least teach us how to pronounce the name:—

'Is there a spot more lovely than the rest,
By art improved, by nature truly blest?
A noble river at its base is running,
It is a little village known as Sonning.'

The present lock-keeper at Sonning does not keep bees and knows nothing of their ways. But on the day before we left our mooring above the lock there was consternation among the patrons of the pleasant little tea garden which adjoins the lock-house and overlooks the weir stream. The air was suddenly filled with bees. A tall dark column of bees whirled and writhed overhead like the vortex of a whirlwind. Finally, they swarmed in a great brown cluster like an elongated swallow's nest, hanging from the cross bar of some trelliswork by the back door of the lock-house. Had folk memory brought them back in quest of their old master? It was a fanciful but happy thought.

22   Henley-on-Thames, Oxfordshire, 1818

From a watercolour by George Shepherd

In the Ashmolean Museum, Oxford

Chapter Four

READING TO OXFORD

NEAR the head of the wide reach between Sonning and Caversham Lock, Reading, the River Kennet enters. Above the junction of this important tributary, the Thames never again achieves quite the same majestic breadth as it does in the lower reaches. The Kennet was made navigable to Newbury under an Act of 1715. Involving the construction of long artificial cuts and many locks, it was one of the most ambitious navigation works of its day and was bitterly opposed by the townspeople of Reading, who feared that they would thereby lose much of their trade to Newbury. In the canal age the Kennet and Avon Canal joined the head of the old navigation with the Bristol Avon, and thus linked the Thames with the Bristol Channel. Even in the Middle Ages the Kennet was navigable to Reading High Bridge. Probably the monks of Reading Abbey were responsible for this work, for in an agreement of 1404 between the Abbey and the town the former grants permission for boats to use the river between sunrise and sunset provided their crews "make no play, riott or noyse". The same document refers to lock tolls, so presumably there was a flash lock on or near the site of the present Blakes Lock— the only lock maintained and staffed by the Thames Conservancy which is not upon the Thames.

Reading Abbey, at first Cluniac but later Benedictine, was once one of the largest in England. The memory of this great house is perpetuated, not by the meagre and pathetic fragments in Forbury Gardens but by one unknown monk who, in the gladness of the spring of the year, was moved to sing "Summer is icumen in, sing cuckoo!" one of the earliest flowers of English poetry, whose freshness has never faded.

Like the stones of its Abbey the remnants of old Reading are few and far between. They have been overwhelmed by the great red town of seeds and biscuits which grew up during the nineteenth century. How great and how rapid that growth was may be judged from the fact that in 1801 the population of the town was under 10,000. In 1948 it was 113,690.

A new bridge has been built across the river just above Caversham Lock, the original Caversham Bridge, which occupies the approximate position of the ancient mediæval bridge, being some distance further upstream. Beyond it, houses and bungalows line the riverside nearly all the way to Tilehurst station, where the Great Western main line runs close beside the river until the latter swings northwards towards Mapledurham Lock. This once lovely reach between the railway and Mapledurham has been marred by a field full of caravans and shacks reminiscent of Walton Bridge or Hurley. But happily this was the last of these outcrops which we were destined to see. There may be occasional blemishes, but no mushroom settlement of magnitude occurs on the river between Mapledurham and Thames Head.

Once this squalid encampment is passed it is easily forgotten, for the prospect ahead is a fair one. Just beyond the lock-cut the river curves beneath the slopes of the Chilterns which, from this point onwards to Goring Gap, march closely beside the Oxfordshire bank. To the right, in the direction of the weir stream, lies Mapledurham House and the Mill, one of the oldest on the river and certainly the most celebrated both in print and in paint. Throughout its history the Tudor manor house has been the property of the Catholic family of Blount, who have a private chapel in the parish church. Thus the old and the reformed faiths share the same building, a rare example of religious toleration.

From Mapledurham we sailed past Hardwick House on its wooded slopes and so down the fine straight reach to Whitchurch Lock. This takes its name from the village on the Oxfordshire bank and ignores its up-and-coming neighbour Pangbourne, whose growth was doubtless initiated by the coming of the Great Western Railway. Beyond the lock, where the Oxford road runs beside the river, Pangbourne exhibits some good examples of that Thames-side Edwardian architecture to which I have already alluded. Then the river leaves the road and there follows another long, straight reach which, in my estimation, surpasses Cliveden. Here, as at Cliveden, wooded slopes, Coombe Park and Hartstock wood, rise steeply from the river to face the level watermeadows on the opposite bank. But whereas at Cliveden we had felt we were passing a somewhat self-conscious 'beauty-spot', preserved within London's orbit, here, despite the proximity of Pangbourne, was beauty of a more natural order. We were now in the country and not in an encircled park. Midway along this reach small islets mark the site of the old flash lock called Hart's. These old locks were often called after their keepers, and as Hart is one of several family names which frequently recur in the history of the Thames, there are, or were, no less than eight places or stations on the river to which the name Hart became attached, a circumstance which must have created some confusion.

To anyone unfamiliar with the Thames valley the term 'Goring Gap' is misleading. It suggests a deep and narrow defile such as the Severn makes at Ironbridge and Coalport, where it cuts its way out of the Vale of Shrewsbury between the Wrekin and Wenlock Edge. On a contoured map it is apparent that the Thames has indeed forced a similar, and, by comparison with the rest of its course, narrow passage through the chalk of the Chilterns and the Berkshire Downs. Indeed, if some geological theories are to be believed, the parallel between the two rivers is close. For just as the Severn originally flowed to join the Dee before it assumed its present

23   St. Peter's Church with Castle in the Background,   Wallingford,   Berkshire

From an aquatint by Robert Havell, 1811

course as a result of geological upheavals, so the Thames joined the Great Ouse on its course to the Wash before, millions of years ago, it carved the chalk. But to the river traveller the Thames 'gap' is not so readily apparent. It has a broad floor of meadows along which the river winds, hugging the high ground now upon one side, now upon the other. Thus by Basildon village and Gatehampton ferry the river crosses from the Chiltern slopes to those of the Moulsford Downs above Streatley.

The twin villages of Goring and Streatley, linked by their long bridge, mark the site of what was, perhaps, the most ancient of all the crossings of the Thames. For it is here that the ancient Ridgeway falls into the valley after its long and lonely march from Avebury over windy downlands starred with the camps and sepulchres of those forgotten men who once travelled it. North of the river it climbs to the upland chalk once more, following the Chiltern escarpment to Dunstable Down and so on into East Anglia. How did Downland man actually cross the river? Probably it was readily fordable except in time of flood. As late as the end of the nineteenth century, it is interesting to find a writer remarking, in quite another connection, upon the shallowness of the river here. "When there was a ferry at Streatley", he says, "persons have been known to ride from Goring to Streatley through the Thames; and on one occasion a person drove through in a one-horse chaise."

Goring and Cleeve Locks were built simultaneously in 1783, the reach between them being the shortest on the river. The six and a half miles between Cleeve and Benson Locks, on the other hand, is the longest unobstructed reach on the non-tidal Thames. It was not always so; there were once two flash locks on the reach, one at Moulsford which, like Hart's, is still marked by the small islets just above the railway bridge, and another called Chalmore Hole a little below Wallingford. Moulsford flash lock had been demolished by the end of the eighteenth century, but a pound-lock was substituted at Chalmore in 1838. It was described as a 'summer or low water lock', all gates being opened and no tolls levied, as at Bray, whenever there was a good flow. Despite petitions from the people of Wallingford, the lock was finally demolished in 1883.

We spent a night on this long reach moored beside the 'Beetle & Wedge' Hotel, where a new management has thoughtfully provided liberal mooring facilities for visiting craft. We returned this compliment by dining at the hotel. Next morning I was awakened soon after dawn by sounds of furious commotion in the water. The sun had just risen into a cloudless sky to shine upon a world that might have been newly created, so fresh it was, so still, so silent and so sparkling with dew. Except for distant bird song there was no sound but this commotion, which was creating tell-tale ripples to flaw the mirror of the water, from some source close to our stern. Here I saw two moor-hens engaged in what appeared to be mortal combat, a scene which seemed strangely out of keeping, not only with the calm beauty of the morning, but with the character of these usually timid and inoffensive birds. Relying upon their outspread tails for support, they reared out of the water breast to breast, and struck out viciously at each other with their large claws. I would never have believed that a bird which generally contrives to appear faintly ridiculous could look so formidable. However, perhaps this air of menace was more apparent than real, for they suddenly broke off the engagement and swam rapidly away in opposite directions, neither showing any signs of having suffered damage from the furious encounter. Perhaps some ornithologist will tell me that I was merely the witness of a little early morning love-play, but I can only say that the display did not seem to me to be either loving or playful.

The only disturbing feature of the pleasant reach from Moulsford to Wallingford is the distant prospect which it affords of the Berkshire lunatic asylum. This is a nightmare in red brick of so terrifying an aspect that one wonders whether the architect was not among the first candidates for admission.

Unlike Henley or the 'Beetle & Wedge', the old town of Wallingford offers no hospitality to the water traveller. The old Public Wharf just above the bridge offers the only reasonable mooring for large craft, but during the season its very restricted length is monopolised by Salter's steamers. This is a pity, because Wallingford is a fine old town which well repays a visit. We continued on our way upstream to Benson Lock and, having obtained permission from the owner of the property, moored in the weir stream above the lock. From this vantage we visited Wallingford by bus next morning, returning, much more appropriately and pleasantly, by the afternoon steamer.

Wallingford Bridge marks the site of another very ancient and important crossing of the river. Originally, no doubt, this would consist of a ford, as at Streatley, but references to a bridge occur as early as 1153. This was probably a timber structure, for it is commonly said that the present stone bridge was built at the instigation of Richard, King of the Romans, who held Wallingford from 1231 to 1271. Having no less than nineteen arches, it was very similar to old London Bridge before it was built upon, and of almost equal length. It has even been conjectured that the same builder was responsible for both, but, if it is true that the latter was built in 1209, this seems unlikely. Some of the original stonework still remains, although the toll of time and the ravages of men and of flood water have necessitated much rebuilding. Parliamentary cannon caused a great deal of damage, and completely destroyed the old bridge chapel, which bore the lovely name of Mary Grace. In 1809 the three main spans were so seriously damaged by a flood that they had to be completely rebuilt, and at the same time the opportunity was taken to widen the entire bridge on the north side to the extent of seven feet. Robert Havell's aquatint (Figure 23) shows the work of reconstruction proceeding. This picture is also of interest because it depicts in the foreground a pair of typical canal craft of the type evolved for work on Brindley's canals. Twenty-five years before this picture was painted, these long narrow craft would have appeared strange indeed to the eyes of the old school of river bargemen accustomed to the type of up-river barge which features in Figure 21. But the completion of the Thames & Severn and Oxford Canals in 1789–90 brought the 'narrow boats' on to the Thames, and during the nineteenth century they became increasingly common on the Upper River. So much so that in the section devoted to the traffic on the river in his *Life on the Upper Thames* (1875), H. R. Robertson refers to them exclusively. He calls them 'wussers', a term I have never encountered elsewhere, and describes and illustrates their elaborate and unique decoration, which is notable for its absence from illustrations of earlier date.

A third feature of interest in Havell's picture is that St. Peter's Church appears apparently unrebuilt and lacking that curious little 'Gothick' spire which has become Wallingford's river landmark. Yet one authority asserts positively that the church was completely rebuilt in 1769, and the spire added eight years later. Both the bridge work and the boats testify that the picture cannot have been painted as early as this.

I have dealt first with Wallingford's bridge, because the whole history of the town, one of the oldest Royal Boroughs in England, hinges upon the importance of the river crossing and the strategic necessity of protecting it. The absence of defensive works at Streatley suggests that the Downland Men who used the Ridgeway were peaceable folk, and that the old road from the Wiltshire Plain to the flint mines of East Anglia had already become archaic as a trade route by the time the Romans came to Britain. The emphasis had shifted upstream to the ford of the Wallingas, 'the sons of the Welsh', on the road to the West, a crossing successively disputed and defended by Celt, Roman, Saxon, Dane and Norman and in the later campaigns between Stephen and Matilda, Royalist and Roundhead. The all-conquering Danish invaders of 871 captured the crossing, but soon afterwards met their first defeat at the hands of King Alfred and his Wessex men on the nearby field of Ethandune, now called Aston Down. It was this legendary victory of the Christian forces of the Golden Dragon which inspired Chesterton to write his great poem 'The Ballad of the White Horse'. However doubtful it may be historically, an imagination stirred by the poem can readily visualise the scene: the over-confident Danes encamped beside the Icknield Way west of Wallingford; the forces of Wessex moving up by night, with the stealth and sureness born of intimate local knowledge, along the older Ridgeway until they:—

'. . . saw across the plains,
In the twilight high and far and fell,
Like the fiery terraces of hell,
The camp fires of the Danes.'

The old defensive ramparts of Wallingford which can still be seen in Kine Croft and Bull Croft remain to remind us of these pre-Conquest days, just as the remnants of Robert d'Oilli's great castle remain the symbol of the later power of the Norman. Held for the King in the Civil War, the castle surrendered to Fairfax after a sixteen weeks' siege and was then almost totally demolished. The little summer house which now occupies the site of the central stronghold on the Norman Motte seems

47

to set the seal to the latter-day peace which has fallen on Wallingford if not upon the world.

The ancient town ramparts, together with the river on the fourth side, form an almost perfect rectangle divided symmetrically in four by the intersection at right-angles of Wallingford's two main thoroughfares. The earthworks are said to be of Celtic origin, but this plan is typical of stereotyped Roman town-planning as exemplified at Silchester and elsewhere. It seems clear that in the south arm of the cross Wallingford once possessed a street of noble breadth, but that subsequent building has split it in two except for the Market Place, where the fine seventeenth-century Town Hall and St. Mary's Church must formerly have stood alone. Walling-ford today is therefore a town of narrow streets, ill fitted for their burden of modern traffic, and of fine examples of Georgian architecture, such as Calleva House near the bridge, rubbing shoulders with buildings of older origin such as its three fine old inns 'The White Hart', 'The Lamb' and, most notably, 'The George'. As we explored the town we remarked a modern 'Before and After' sign which appealed to us hanging outside a barber's shop in St. Mary's street. Upon one side it portrayed a worried-looking gentleman with tousled hair and hirsute chin; on the other the same gentleman smooth-chinned and glossy, having obviously left his worries behind with his superfluous hair. Beneath was the enigmatic inscription: "Two heads are better than one.—Old Saying." We could do with more such original signs of local inspiration and execution to enliven our streets. But perhaps they would offend the tidy minds of the town planners.

When they reach Benson, the Thames guide-book writers unanimously insist that their readers must leave the river to visit Ewelme. This seems a little unfair. For although Ewelme is undoubtedly a very lovely village, whereas Benson is not particularly noteworthy, the single main street of Bensington (as it used to be called) is very pleasant and peaceful. It is a real village street with no false pretensions about it and includes a village shop which exhibits a wonderful variety of stock. The main road by-pass has certainly brought quiet to Benson, though it may have damaged the business of its two large inns. Unfortunately, however, having got rid of its motor-traffic problem, Benson is now being assaulted from the air. While we were moored there, aircraft from the neighbouring aerodrome droned overhead all night long as they practised night landing.

We left our mooring in the weir stream at Benson on the morning of a day of great heat and soon saw Shillingford Bridge ahead of us. Built in 1827 to replace an earlier bridge of timber on stone piers, it is a three-arched structure of remarkable grace, the most graceful, perhaps, on the whole course of the Thames. It is favoured, too, in its situation beneath the steep tree covered slopes of the Berkshire bank. Unfortunately, the beauty of the place has induced a popularity which at times becomes too great to appeal to those unsociable and undemocratic people who seek solitude. The attractive Swan Inn which overlooks the bridge has long ago changed its name to the Shillingford Bridge Hotel, while there are hutments dotted about

24 Abingdon, Berkshire, *circa* 1820

From a watercolour by George Shepherd

In the Ashmolean Museum, Oxford

which are, I believe, euphemistically called chalets. A numerous company were disporting themselves on the riverside lawns and in the water as we passed, while a noisy motor launch was towing one scantily clad maiden up and down the river on water skis.

The bridge was soon passed, and as we held steadily on our way past Keen Edge Ferry and the mouth of the Thame to Day's Lock we thought the river was remarkably quiet, considering the perfect weather and the fact that it was a Sunday. By the time we reached the lock it was high noon and the heat was so intense that we decided to travel no further. We found a mooring at the head of the weir by the tip of the narrow peninsula dividing it from the lock-cut, and were soon cooling off in the river.

So far we had not visited many of the Thames valley churches, for with but few notable exceptions the hand of the nineteenth-century restorer has been heavy upon them. But despite the heat of the day we took the field path that leads from the lock and past the mysterious Dyke Hills into Dorchester in order to see the Abbey Church of SS. Peter and Paul, the mediæval successor to the Saxon Cathedral of St. Birinus. Unlike Benson, Dorchester has not been by-passed. The funereal tarmac of the main road was hot and sticky under foot, and a procession of cars was buzzing across the long bridge over the Thame and between the fine old houses which line the winding village street. But once inside the great church, which is withdrawn from the road among the trees of its graveyard, it was cool and quiet, the noonday glare softened or broken into kaleidoscopic patterns in its passage through superb mediæval glass.

The visitor enters the Abbey by the south aisle and the first impression is disappointing. A curtain wall, a relic of the days when the church was divided between monks and villagers, cuts off the view of the east end. But move across into the Nave and there, through the Early English Chancel arch, is the glory of Dorchester's Chancel and Sanctuary; the great east window; the famous Jesse window with its unique sculptured tracery; the lovely fourteenth-century triple sedilia. The whole is an unrivalled example of English Gothic craftsmanship at the full height and vigour of its powers.

But what most impressed me at Dorchester was the contrast between two altar tombs in the South Aisle. Upon one of them lies the alabaster effigy of a knight of the Seagrave family clad in chain mail whose every interlocking link has been faithfully carved out. It is a feat of patient and meticulous craftsmanship that is oriental in its painstaking quality. The whole effect, too, is of an oriental passivity. This knight is sleeping; calmly, and with neither hope nor fear, he has lain him down to rest for all eternity. That armour which once rang with the buffets of the world has turned into a winding sheet of stone. No single one of those thousand links will ever ring or clink again to restless movement; petrified, they hold him like bands of mummy cloth, closely, in perpetual stillness.

Nearby is one of the most remarkable monuments to be seen in any church. It is

49

the tomb of an unknown knight. Four hundred years ago it was recorded that: "His name is out of remembrance" and yet he remains terribly, supernaturally alive. No work in stone that I have seen achieves such vitality and dynamic energy as the effigy of this nameless warrior. For this knight, death holds no repose. He is recumbent, but, like legendary Arthur and his knights beneath their hill in Camelot, he waits century by century for some unknown signal, tensed, eternally vigilant. The muscles of his crossed legs are strung and poised upon the brink of sudden swift and certain action; one arm he has flung across his body in a single urgent and unerring arc of movement to grip the hilt of his sword. Already he has eased it from its sheath. Even the lion that crouches at his feet seems roused to spring, like a dog who senses his master's expectant purpose. What does he await, this unknown knight? The Second Coming? If the last trump should suddenly cry upon Sinodun, surely that sword would flash singing from its scabbard, those mailed heels clash upon the stone? But Seagrave would still sleep sound.

On our way out across the South Aisle I paused to read the inscription upon a slab on the floor. It commemorated a Mrs. Sarah Fletcher who died in 1799 at the age of twenty-nine and read:—

> Reader!
> If thou hast a heart formed for
> Tenderness and pity, Contemplate
> this Spot
> In which are deposited the Remains
> of a Young Lady, whose artless Beauty,
> innocence of Mind, and gentle Manners
> once obtained her the Love and
> Esteem of all who knew her, but when
> nerves were too delicately spun to
> Bear the rude Shakes and Jostlings
> which we meet within this transitory
> World, Nature gave way; she sank
> and died a Martyr to Excessive
> Sensibility. . . .
> May her soul meet that peace in heaven.
> which this earth denied her.

In this cynical and hard-boiled age there are many who may find poor Mrs. Fletcher's Excessive Sensibility somewhat ludicrous. Yet is it not poignant? All those who lack either the resignation or the pugnacity of Mrs. Fletcher's attendant knights will surely understand her suffering in the long night of the world and hope that her soul has indeed found peace.

If I were asked what point on the Thames between Oxford and the sea most appealed to me I would not hesitate to choose the neighbourhood of Day's Lock, where the river curves close under Long Wittenham Wood and the slopes of Sinodun.

In the cool of the evening as the sun was setting I crossed the footbridge over the weir stream, followed the steep track past Little Wittenham Church, and climbed towards the twin hills of Sinodun, each wearing its crown of trees—the Wittenham Clumps—which make them so prominent a landmark of the Oxfordshire vale. The more westerly of the two hills bears no evidence of any defensive works but, beneath the trees, its crown is quite flat and circular, as though levelled and prepared for the celebration of some unknown ceremonial. The summit of the other hill is ringed by a great defensive ditch and rampart. I stood first on one and then on the other of these outliers of the chalk. The sun went down, and the Vale of the White Horse began to fill with darkness. Did the men who reared this rampart look with friendly or hostile eyes across this vale to the long downland skyline where similar camps gazed back at Sinodun? And, looking northwards now across the silver shining Thames below Wittenham Wood, what was the purpose of the great dyke enclosing the angle of the river, when a hill fort such as this was so close at hand? Was it an outer defence of the fort, or was it thrown up by some opposing force? Neither seems a likely answer. So enigmatic and mysterious are the memorials that Downland man has left upon his lonely hills, that imagination stands as good a chance of hitting the truth as the patient spade of the archæologist. He can group them into cultures of his own naming but he cannot make them live. I like to think that just as thrushes sing on a May morning or as a flock of starlings wheels and swings in an autumn sky, so the people who flattened the crown of western Sinodun danced there in the sunlight of the morning of the world.

From Day's Lock the Thames describes a great arc through the meadows to the pleasant little riverside village of Clifton Hampden with its nineteenth-century brick bridge, beyond which is Clifton Lock and cut. A lock was proposed at Clifton in 1793, but the work was not completed until 1822, one legal reason for the delay being the curious fact that the owner of the requisite land turned out to be a lunatic.

A straight and rather uninteresting reach leads from Clifton Cut under ugly Appleford railway bridge to the deep lock at Culham with its narrow bridge and long cut. Prior to the opening of this lock and cut in 1809, the navigation followed the main course of the river by the old and beautiful village of Sutton Courtenay, where was situated a very curious lock which illustrates the transition from the flash to the pound lock. This was built at some unknown date in the latter half of the seventeenth century, although a sixteenth-century writer refers to two flash locks here, a fact which suggests that some similar arrangement existed even at this early date. The seventeenth-century lock was, indeed, often referred to in the plural, for it consisted, in effect, of two flash locks set one at the head and one at the tail of the large pool behind old Sutton Mill, which thus became the lock pound. A less convenient arrangement would be hard to conceive. The pound naturally took a very long time to fill or to empty and consumed in the process a prodigious volume of water. This seriously interfered with the working of the mill, whose owners consequently levied an exceptionally heavy toll on the barge traffic. Moreover, to make matters worse, the upper set of gates were actually under the floor of the mill and a writer in 1782 complained that: "There is a kind of pound at Sutton Mills, but the Timbers of the floor of the House under which Barges pass are too low when the Water is tolerable high, so that it is not easy to pass thro'." After the present Culham lock had obviated this ancient hazard, the Commissioners for the Upper Thames bought up the old lock and its tolls for £3,000.

The course of the Thames and its navigation in the neighbourhood of Abingdon have undergone some interesting changes in the course of time. At the head of Culham Reach, where the river bends sharply in the direction of this old Berkshire town, the towpath may be seen to bridge the mouth of an inconspicuous backwater, much overgrown, which continues the line of the Reach. This backwater, which is known as the Swift Ditch, leaves the river half a mile from Abingdon Lock and encloses between it and the present course of the river an expanse of meadowland which is known as Andersey Island. If tradition, as recorded by Leland and others, is correct, this insignificant backwater once formed the sole course of the Thames until the monks of Abingdon diverted the river for the 'convenience and cleanliness' of their Abbey. This piece of ancient monastic engineering now forms the most northerly channel of the river at Abingdon and is called the Abbey stream. In or about 1060, however, the present navigation channel was dug between the upper and lower partings of the Abbey Stream. In 1624, the Oxford–Burcot Commission was formed to improve the navigation of the river between Oxford and Culham and decided that the Swift Ditch should become the main line of navigation. In this way the ancient course of the river acquired a new lease of life. At Iffley, at Sandford and near the head of the Swift Ditch, this enterprising body built pound-locks which were among the earliest in England. The first two have, of course, long been rebuilt, but the old chamber of the Swift Ditch Lock, much overgrown and dammed at the lower end, remains as evidence that these locks were of very substantial and durable construction. They were by no means improvisations such as the old lock at Sutton Courtenay, and would seem to have been far superior to the locks built further down the river under the Act of 1770, which appear to have been largely of timber construction and to have required rebuilding within a very few years. The stone walls of the Old Swift Ditch Lock, on the other hand, are a beautiful piece of mason's work, the chamber measuring, according to Thacker, approximately 80 feet by 20 feet. In 1790, Abingdon Lock was constructed on the present site, so that for the second time the old Swift Ditch became a forgotten backwater, and the navigation reverted to the mediæval channel.

We moored in the meadows just below Abingdon (Figures 24, 25) and spent a considerable time exploring and admiring this remarkable town. Despite the fact that the motor industry which has industrialised Oxford has invaded Abingdon also, I do not consider that any other town in the Thames valley has retained its individual and historical character in the way that Abingdon has done. It is impossible to stand

25 The Bridge and Church at Abingdon, Berkshire

From an aquatint by Robert Havell, 1811

anywhere in this old town and fail to see at least one noteworthy building. I hope this praise will do no harm, for the charm of Abingdon resides in the fact that it does not appear to be in the least self-conscious, although with such a historical heritage and such a riverside site it might easily have become so. It remains a worka-day country town going busily about its immemorial business, like an active veteran who scorns to live on charity but insists on paying his own way. Such liveliness in old towns sometimes leads to 'improvements' which the lover of the past deplores, but it is at least arguable that life, even at this price, is preferable to the preservation of a beauty from which life has departed and which is therefore no longer allied to function. If our modern way of life had not become implacably hostile to beauty in architecture, as in any other applied art, there would not be any problem here or any need for an army of preservationists.

The only building we saw in Abingdon which has been preserved in the full sense of the word, and rightly so, is the surviving fragment of the great Benedictine Abbey of St. Mary the Virgin which brought the town into being. The Abbey Church, 370 feet long and 170 feet across the transepts, was destroyed with such extraordinary diligence at the dissolution that even the foundations were dug out. With the exception of the gatehouse, all that survived was a portion of the domestic buildings which, for the most part, had become slum property ripe for demolition when it was acquired by 'The Friends of Abingdon'. This enterprising local body, with the assistance of the Pilgrim Trust, has set about the task of restoration. The most important part of this acquisition consists of the Chequer (or Exchequer) of the Abbey with an adjoining partitioned long gallery where, presumably, the clerks once worked. The Chequer possesses a fine fireplace connected to a tall, capped thirteenth-century chimney which is unique in England. When 'The Friends' have completed their admirable work of restoration it will fittingly record the fact that the town once possessed one of the richest and most powerful monastic houses in mediæval England.

The most interesting secular building in Abingdon, if not on all Thames-side, is Christ's Hospital at St. Helen's Wharf on the river's edge. An almshouse for the aged and infirm, this Hospital was founded in the fifteenth century by one of the two Abingdon Guilds, the Fraternity of the Holy Cross. Historical records prove, unfortunately, that the rule of the great Abbey at this period was despotic, and, as a result of the unpopularity so caused, the Guild became the recipient of endowments which might otherwise have gone to the Abbey. These enabled it to build the oldest of the present buildings, which is now known as the Long Alley. Certain alterations, notably the addition of porches and alterations to the Governors' Hall, were carried out at the beginning of the seventeenth century, but otherwise this long, low, galleried building with its tall chimneys and graceful central lantern remains sub-stantially as it was when it was built in 1446. Moreover, it is still serving the purpose for which it was built, under the beneficent rule of its Master and Governors, a circumstance fully in keeping with the character of Abingdon. It is a rule that was set up in 1553 when Christ's Hospital was created by Royal Charter five years after the Guild of the Holy Cross was suppressed.

Overlooking Long Alley and the later and equally attractive Georgian buildings of the Hospital is Abingdon's most prominent building—St. Helen's Church, whose tall spire features in every picture of the town and is familiar to every Thames traveller (Figures 24, 25). The interior is peculiar because it is broader than it is long, the nave having five aisles. But it has been much restored and is chiefly remarkable for the superb painted ceiling of the chancel and for some fine eighteenth-century brass candelabra.

Another of Abingdon's fine buildings which must be mentioned is the imposing Market Hall, completed in 1683 by Christopher Kempster to a design by Wren. A spacious square enables its admirable proportions to be properly appreciated.

At the lower end of St. Helen's Wharf the little River Ock flows in to the Thames. Here was formerly the junction of the Wilts & Berks Canal, which ran westwards through the Vale of the White Horse to join the Kennet & Avon Canal at Semington near Devizes. It was finally abandoned in 1914, and when I paused to investigate on our way back to our boat from Christ's Hospital I could find no trace of the actual junction with the river. A hundred yards or so inland, however, its filled-in course became apparent. The canal formed another link between the Thames and the Severn, and if the project to extend it eastwards to Aylesbury had taken shape, Abingdon might have become quite an important centre of inland navigation.

The same Guild which was responsible for the Long Alley almshouses also built, earlier in the same century, the river bridges at Abingdon and Culham, the former replacing an earlier timber bridge. The main spans of Abingdon Bridge have been rebuilt in recent years, but some of the Guild's work survives at the northern end. Within sight of the bridge upstream is Abingdon Lock, where the old Abbey Stream leaves the main channel and where the river traveller heads out into open country once again.

Immediately the ugly Nuneham railway bridge is passed, a lovely reach opens out beneath the wooded slopes of Nuneham Park, a reach punctuated by an attractive and much photographed island which is linked to the park by a rustic bridge. The navigation channel now passes the island on the Berkshire side, but the old channel took the opposite course, beneath the bridge, where there was originally a flash lock, the property of Lord Harcourt. There was a proposal, in 1788, to build a pound-lock here, but nothing came of it. The old lock finally went out of use about 1800, but the cottage by the bridge is still known as 'Lock Cottage' and the wood above it as 'Lock Wood'.

Soon after this island has been rounded, Nuneham Park itself comes into view, a curious Palladian mansion consisting of two great grey wings linked by a low corridor. The estate was the property of the Courtenay family from the thirteenth century until 1710, when it was bought by Simon Harcourt, of Stanton Harcourt, Lord Chancellor of England. In the process of enclosing the park, the entire village

54

of Nuneham was swept away and a new village, Nuneham Courtney, built on the main Oxford–Henley road 'beyond the pale'. On the highest point of the park stands the Carfax, Oxford's old conduit house, which was removed thither when the High was widened in 1787.

From the western boundary of Nuneham Park and the Radley boathouses there follows a somewhat dull reach to Sandford Lock, the river running between high banks and level fields, the chimney of Sandford Mill visible in the distance but never seeming to draw nearer. Sandford has the distinction of being the deepest lock on the river, the fall being as much as 8 feet 6 inches in times of low water. John Taylor, the water poet, mentions the original lock, built by the Oxford–Burcot Commission, as being in use in 1632. It was lengthened in 1793 and rebuilt two years later, but in 1836 a new lock was opened beside it on the present site. In 1881 the owners of the mill, the Clarendon Press, purchased the old pound-lock to form a headrace for an additional mill wheel, and as such its fabric is still to be seen, although, owing to the eighteenth-century reconstruction, it is not of the same historical interest as the old lock on the Swift Ditch. Sandford Paper Mill today has a very busy, prosaic and factory-like appearance, but it has a very ancient history, having been built in 1294 by the Knights Templar who had a preceptory nearby.

Of the short reach between Sandford and Iffley Locks there is little to be said except to mention the very acute turns which the river makes as it rounds the small island known variously as St. Michael's, Kennington, or Rose Island. Iffley Lock is as shallow as Sandford is deep, having an average fall of only 2 feet 9 inches. Its removal, and the deepening of the channel up to Osney, has been advanced as a flood preventing measure, but the lock remains on the site of its seventeenth-century predecessor. Iffley village is, or was, a pleasant place with a remarkably fine Norman church, but the suburbs of swollen Oxford have crept out and enveloped it.

We moored for the night in Iffley Reach, near the new reinforced-concrete footbridge which leaps arrogantly across the river in a single lofty span. The megaphonic cries of coaches encouraging or admonishing their practising crews echoed over the water, but the towpath opposite us was so thronged with evening strollers that the coaches were having the utmost difficulty in keeping up with their boats. As I watched their bicycles weaving in and out through a crowd which made little attempt to give way to them, I thought the spectacle symptomatic of the losing battle which the Gown seems to be fighting against the ever-growing Town. Nowhere is the crass affront, the blank negation which the 'culture' of twentieth-century industrialism presents to the English tradition of a thousand years more apparent than in modern Oxford, once one of the fairest of all English cities.

'Towery city and branchy between towers;
Cuckoo-echoing, bell-swarmèd, lark-charmèd, rook-racked, river-rounded,
The dapple-eared lily below thee; that country and town did
Once encounter in, here coped and poised powers;

55

Thou hast a base and brickish skirt there, sours
That neighbour-nature thy grey beauty is grounded
Best in; graceless growth, thou hast confounded
Rural rural keeping—folk, flocks and flowers.' *

That base and brickish skirt has spread in far greater and more graceless growth since Hopkins' day, and the plight of the towery city of stone is symbolic of the twilight of Western Christendom. It has become a citadel of the humanities cut off and sorely beset. The encircling hosts may have paid their way with money, but no such lip-service however lavish can restore lost peace or that lovely, gracious poise; that marriage of field and stone which Hopkins celebrated but which the besiegers have never known and cannot understand. The thundering traffic, the crowds that overflow the pavements, they have destroyed forever those 'golden Oxford afternoons' that all might once discover. The loss may be imponderable, but it is of a magnitude unmeasurable.

* From *Duns Scotus's Oxford* by Gerard Manley Hopkins

The Manor House, Kelmscott, Oxfordshire

From a drawing by E. H. New

26   Oxford from Wytham Hill

Photographed by the Earl of Mayo, from the painting by William Turner

Chapter Five

OXFORD TO THAMES HEAD

FROM Iffley Lock as far as Folly Bridge the Thames prospect is comparatively unsullied. Here is the mouth of the tree-shaded Cherwell, whose source at Hellidon on the Daventry Wolds is closely shared by the rivers Nene and Leam which flow to the Wash and the Bristol Channel. Here, too, along the bank of Christ Church Meadow, is the line of College Barges. Some of these lovely, ornate craft, which were once the State Barges of the City Companies, look sadly dilapidated today. But they have become such an institution, and make so notable and unique a contribution to Oxford's river, that one might have assumed that their restoration would be a foregone conclusion. But no, apparently the City Fathers in their infinite wisdom have decreed that they are insanitary and must be replaced by permanent structures on the bank. If the appearance of most of the so-called 'permanent structures' erected today be any criterion, this sacrifice to modern hygiene is hardly likely to improve the appearance of the river or of Christ Church Meadow. The fate of the College Barges is similar to that of the little man in the old *Punch* cartoon who, because his chimney is on fire, is being arraigned by a large policeman while in the background a row of belching factory chimneys darken the sky. For the most dilapidated and insanitary of barges is a thing of beauty when compared with the City's own riverside properties, which vomit smoke and stench over the river beyond Folly Bridge.

The first bridge at this point of which there is record, and certainly the first stone bridge, was built about 1085 by Robert d'Oilli of Wallingford and Oxford Castles. It was called South Bridge or Grand Pont until the seventeenth century, when the tenant of a little building, probably originally a defensive work, at the north end of the bridge earned it the title of 'Folly'. This building, which had become known as 'Friar Bacon's Study', was demolished in 1779. Beneath the narrow arches of the bridge there was a flash weir, a combination so obstructive to navigation that the language of the unfortunate bargemen negotiating this hazard became almost proverbial. Between 1820 and 1828 the bridge was completely rebuilt, the weir tackle removed, and a shallow pound-lock constructed for use in times of low water. In 1884 the lock gates were taken away and the lock channel opened out, but the chamber walls can still be seen. Through-traffic usually takes this narrow channel, thus avoiding the congestion of steamers and boats which is usually to be found by Salter's Yard on the main channel just below the bridge.

Above Folly Bridge the scene changes with dramatic suddenness, and the river traveller is greeted with a spectacle which is happily without parallel anywhere else on the whole course of the river between Thames Head and the sea. The scale of London River is too big to be wholly marred by anything that can be built upon its banks, but in any case London also has her embankments and fine riverside buildings. Kingston, Staines and Reading each insult the Thames in one way or another, but they do not ignore her. Only Oxford has seen fit to turn its back upon the river and use it as a squalid backyard. As the river winds through the heart of a gasworks and past mean streets and railway yards it is easy for the traveller to imagine that he has been magically transported to the waters of some Black Country canal. Beyond the main railway bridge there is a brief respite as far as Osney Lock, but as the water rises in the lock there comes into view more of that 'base and brickish skirt' and, crowning insult, the waterside power station where once the Abbey of Osney stood.

However sadly Thames' banks have been despoiled hereabouts in the nineteenth and twentieth centuries, it must in fairness be admitted that the river itself is much cleaner than it was in the seventeenth if John Taylor's remarkable verse is to be believed. In 1644 the water poet found himself penniless at Oxford and took on the job of River Inspector. He described this experience as follows:—

> 'Then by the Lords Commissioners, and also
> By my good King (whom all true subjects call so)
> I was commanded with the Water Baylie
> To see the Rivers clensed, both night and dayly.
> Dead Hogges, Dogges, Cates and well flayd Carryon Horses,
> Their noysom Corpses soyld the Water Courses;
> Both swines and Stable dunge, Beasts guts and Garbage,
> Street durt, with Gardners weeds and Rotten Herbage.
> And from those Waters filthy putrification,
> Our meat and drinke were made, which bred Infection.
> My self and partner, with cost paines and Travell,
> Saw all made clean, from Carryon, Mud and Gravell;
> And now and then was punisht a Deliquent,
> By which good meanes away the filth and stink went.'

Taylor's ability to coerce a rhyme makes the metrical efforts of old Mr. Sadler, the bee-keeper of Sonning, pale into insignificance, but he seems to have performed a formidable task on the Thames. That work is now carried on with great zeal and conspicuous success by the Thames Conservancy. On the tidal river the writ of the Anti-Pollution laws does not run, but above Teddington no great river is better protected from pollution. In this good cause stringent by-laws prevent the discharge and disposal of waste from craft using the river, but in this case they would prove more effectual if the unfortunate boat-owner could be provided with some adequate

27   Witney, Coggs, and the River Windrush, Oxfordshire, *circa* 1820
(The Octagonal Tower of Coggs Church can be seen on the left)

From a watercolour by George Shepherd

In the Ashmolean Museum, Oxford

facilities for shore disposal at locks or other specified points on the river. He does his best, because it is in his own best interests so to do, but he is not a camel, neither can he equip his boat with a refuse destructor.

In the vicinity of Oxford the Thames breaks into a maze of streams, and the history of the navigation through the city resembles that of Abingdon. Most westerly of all is the channel formed by the Wytham, or Seacourt, and the Hinksey Streams. Between them these two streams form a long, narrow backwater which extends from Hagley Pool, above King's Lock, to the neighbourhood of Kennington Island below Iffley, thus by-passing the whole of the city. Little more than a dyke in places, it was surveyed in the eighteenth century with a view to making it the navigation channel. The old line of navigation through Oxford followed the eastern channel of the river from Medley Weir to Hithe Bridge and Castle Mill, rejoining the present navigation at Preacher's Pool where the gasworks now stand. It is with this stream that the Oxford Canal makes a junction at Isis or Louse Lock, craft bound for the river using the short connecting link under the railways to Four Streams above Osney Bridge. Tradition has it that the present navigation from Medley Weir to Preacher's Pool was originally engineered by the monks of Osney for the purpose of driving the Abbey mill and doubtless, as at Abingdon, 'for the convenience and cleanliness' of the Abbey itself.

It requires a considerable effort of imagination today to envisage that mediæval city which Wycliffe was moved to call the Vineyard of the Lord. Magnificent Osney, one of the greatest and proudest monastic houses in Europe; the lesser Rewley Abbey; the Cathedral; the schools of the Regular and Mendicant Orders which were the foundation of the University; the great Norman castle; all 'watered by rills and fountains, surrounded by meadows, pastures, plains and glades'. All have been swept away, and only the great bell of Osney still sonorously tolls away the hours from Tom Tower in Christ Church.

The original Osney Bridge was built by the monks, and its arches were so narrow that barges frequently became jammed in it. In 1885 the central span collapsed and the present single-span iron bridge was completed in 1889. For some reason difficult to understand, considering its comparatively modern date, the headroom provided beneath it is much less than that of any other bridge on the navigable Thames. It excludes many boats from the upper river, while in times of high water it becomes impassable for craft of any size. Once this bridge is passed that unhappy chapter of the river's course which begins at Folly Bridge is closed. We soon found ourselves heading away from Oxford's unsightly outskirts and railway yards towards Medley Weir and Port Meadow.

Until well into the present century, flash locks survived at Medley and King's Weir. In their final form they were not of the old paddle and rimer type, but each consisted of a single pair of opening gates moved against the stream by winches after the same fashion as the two single gate weirs which still stand on the Warwick Avon at Pershore and Cropthorne. Even so, as anyone who has used the Avon weirs will appreciate, they must have been extremely slow to negotiate, and from 1790 onwards river traffic of suitable dimensions commonly avoided this part of the river by using the Oxford canal between Isis Lock, Oxford, and the Wolvercote Millstream above King's Weir, to which the canal has access via its Duke's Cut Branch. Consequently, it was recorded in 1861 that: ''no Canal Boat or Barge has passed down the said part of the River (with the exception of two or three boats partly loaded with timber and two or three Canal Boats with Coals) during the last two years.'' It was doubtless due to the existence of this alternative route that, despite proposals to build pound-locks, the two weirs survived so long. There is now an open channel at Medley, while a pound-lock has been built at King's.

From Medley to Godstow Lock the river sweeps round the great expanse of Port Meadow in a fine reach of a breadth which is remarkable considering that the river's volume is now much reduced. This Binsey Reach is more in keeping with the character of the Thames below Oxford, a character, ample, stately yet disciplined, which lives up to the hackneyed patronymic 'Father Thames'. But at Binsey the upstream voyager sees the last of this stately and rather sophisticated old gentleman, for above Godstow Lock the river has a totally different and, for me, more attractive character.

Matthew Arnold has often been unkindly criticised for coining the adjectival 'stripling' in 'The Scholar-Gipsy' to describe this upper river. It has been suggested that he selected it, not because it was particularly apposite but because it best served the metre of his verse. Is not this suggestion a little unfair to the poet? The appellation seems overworked and hackneyed now, a pompous whimsy, no more. Yet it was fresh enough when Arnold minted it, and is it so inapt to describe an immature and wayward river? The Thames above Godstow is narrow and for the greater part of its course extremely tortuous. Locks and cuts may have disciplined it at intervals, but between them it pays no stately court to riverside towns and refuses to provide raw material for the landscape gardener. Instead, for mile after winding mile it wanders in willow-bordered solitude through water meadows whose loneliness its own impetuosity assures. For rains which the lower river can easily contain are sufficient to set this young stream straying from its bed and stealing over the fields in shallow but ostentatious spate.

After proposals to build a lock at a point on Binsey Reach mysteriously known as Black Jack's Hole had been discarded, Godstow Lock was built and opened in 1790. With its cut it forms a third channel at this point, the other two being the tail of the old weir channel and the mouth of the Wolvercote Millstream. The upstream end of the last-named not only provides a link with the waterways of the Midlands as already mentioned, but also has the distinction of touching the most northerly point on the whole course of the Thames. Its Mill, like that at Sandford, has a long history but presents a workaday appearance. Like Sandford, too, it is a paper mill owned, in this case, by the Oxford University Press. Here is produced the celebrated 'India Paper' which combines extreme thinness with remarkable opacity and is used most commonly in the production of prayer books and pocket bibles.

The construction of Godstow Lock, by raising the river level, is said to have diminished the value of the land on the Wytham Flats and on the island known as Pixey Mead formed by the Wolvercote Stream. Certainly much of this land is now fenny ground, unprofitable, but in summer an impenetrable bird sanctuary of tall reeds, yellow flags, meadowsweet and other marshland flowers.

Though the suburbs of Oxford have already marched into nearby Wolvercot, they have not yet invaded Godstow. Fenced off from them by the railway, Port Meadow is an inviolate open space, while to the west the country north of Botley is unsullied.

'Where is the girl, who by the boatman's door,
Above the locks, above the boating throng,
Unmoor'd our skiff when through the Wytham flats,
Red loosestrife and blond meadowsweet among,
And darting swallows and light water-gnats,
We track'd the shy Thames shore?'

Where, indeed, is the girl? But the Wytham Flats remain as Arnold recalled them when he wrote his nostalgic lament for lost youth and so, too, does the little stone village of Wytham sheltering under the wooded slopes of its hill (Figure 26). It is therefore still a place to linger in in hot June weather, so when we had cleared Godstow's narrow skew bridge we followed the poet's example and:—

'. . . Moor'd to the cool bank in the summer-heats,
Mid wide grass meadows which the sunshine fills,'
To 'watch the warm green-muffled Cumner hills . . .'

If we search through the stores of memory, it will become apparent to many of us, I think, that the most memorable moments of our lives are not necessarily the occasion of important events or of meetings with people and places whose significance only becomes apparent later. Often when time has blurred our recollection of many things which seemed memorable, the mind will yet retain most vividly the image of the experience of some brief and fortuitous moment. Who can say why this should be so? Unless it be that there are rare occasions when our cabined faculties are for an instant liberated and privileged to apprehend the eternal in the temporal. So it was that an experience during our stay at Godstow, which seems of little account in the telling, will, I know, remain with me most vividly when all other recollections of the Thames have faded. The occasion was merely a bathe in the river at midnight. The last of the patrons of the nearby 'Trout' inn had long ago departed on his noisy way, and the night was not only silent but breathlessly still and very warm. It was also very dark, for the sky was completely overcast. Only in the far west over the river there appeared an occasional swift flicker of summer lightning; not the rending, blinding flash of imminent storm but its pale echo reflected momentarily between cloud and water. This light, whose source was neither moon nor star nor sun, seemed to possess an apocalyptic quality; it suggested that the dark horizon it revealed in such sudden and fleeting chiaroscuro might be no part of our familiar earth, but the rim of some strange world towards which our course was set. And as I swam through the cool water, making as little noise as possible, I experienced a curious feeling, exalting yet at the same time humbling, of becoming for a moment a part of this great river, ever changing yet always the same, eternally dying in the sea because it is eternally renewed.

Within view of our moorings was the site of the Priory of Godstow, traditionally associated with the story of the frail Fair Rosamund—'Rosa Mundi non rosa Munda', but may she rest in peace. Such few fragments of the old Nunnery as remain now form part of the high wall of a rectangular pound, and here we were lucky enough to see a purely mediæval custom enacted. Late one evening our curiosity was thoroughly aroused by sudden signs of some purposeful and discreet—one might almost say furtive—activity, the object of which seemed quite inexplicable. Some policemen together with several gentlemen who, probably unwittingly, radiated an air of official importance, were to be seen strolling about or standing in converse on or near the bridge. Then a party of men arrived with rolls of chestnut-pale fencing and proceeded to erect a fenced way from the field gate on the road-side to the doorway of Godstow Pound. It was only after the event that we realised that preparations were being made for the Sheriff of Oxford's annual drive on Port Meadow. Such preparations have to be both speedy and discreet, for otherwise some of the graziers of Port Meadow might defeat the object of the drive by removing their stock.

At four-forty-five a.m. the following morning, thirteen horsemen, led by the Sheriff, began to round up the stock on the Meadow and at five a.m. the meadow gates were locked. At six o'clock cattle began to enter Godstow Pound and an hour later they had all been impounded with the exception of a few 'singletons' or odd strays which would have become exhausted by further pursuit. After the Sheriff's customary breakfast at Wolvercote village hall, the claiming of beasts by their respective owners began and continued until the afternoon. Freemen of the City of Oxford and Commoners of Wolvercote, who possess ancient grazing rights on Port Meadow, each paid twopence a head for their stock, but those who could not claim this privilege had to pay at least two guineas a head, such money going to the relief of rates. This most ancient annual event has recently been criticised on humanitarian grounds, though none of the animals we saw showed any signs of distress. Some of us are inclined to wax too sentimental about animals at the expense of the immense sum of human misery in the world.

Soon after we had witnessed this impounding ceremony we left our Godstow mooring one bright but breezy afternoon and sailed away up the extremely tortuous reach to King's Lock. Above King's the river which, since Nuneham, has maintained a northerly direction, swings west and south-west on a less devious course as it rounds Wytham Hill (Figure 26), hugging the slopes of Wytham Great Wood in the neighbourhood of Eynsham Bridge. Hereabouts there joins the Thames the Evenlode from Wychwood, and what other English river can boast tributaries with names so lovely and so fitting as Evenlode or Windrush (Figure 27)? A poet might have christened them so, the one a sleepy river, slow, meandering and seeking shade; the other hurrying from the open wolds, clear, murmurous and sparkling in the sunlight.

Close to the mouth of the Evenlode is the entrance to the old Cassington Cut. This is now no more than a brook, but it was once a navigable canal with a lock near its entrance which joined the Evenlode to cut off the last three miles of its tortuous course. What was the purpose of this canal I have not been able to discover, unless it was to serve Eynsham Mills.

Like Kings, Eynsham is a modern lock replacing a navigation weir. Unlike Medley or King's, however, there was no avoiding Eynsham Weir, and Oxford Canal boatmen have regaled me with stories of the awkward and sometimes hazardous task of negotiating it when they were bound up river with coal or returning downstream with hay or stone. Just above the lock is the handsome toll bridge, built by the Earl of Abingdon in 1777, beyond which the river again becomes very tortuous. In the level watermeadows between the bridge and Pinkhill Lock with its fine garden, and again between Pinkhill and Bablockhithe, the Thames does its best to tie itself in knots.

I wish I could describe Bablockhithe in terms appropriate to its beautiful name but, alas, honesty forbids. The rebuilt inn is not particularly attractive, while its immediate surroundings are not improved by a row of week-end 'chalets' and by even more unsightly signs of week-end popularity such as an old double-decker bus. There is also a rope ferry at Bablockhithe which provides a trap for the unwary navigator. To allow craft to pass, the rope must be dropped to the bed of the river, and when not so dropped it hangs close to the surface of the water and is not easily seen. It is true that there are warning boards, but their lettering is faded and they are not conspicuously placed.

Bablockhithe is a very small blemish on this lovely upper river, and the ensuing stretch through Northmoor Lock to New Bridge leaves nothing to be desired. For here the open watermeadows are left behind for a space and there are many trees to provide shade and shelter and variety. Lonely Northmoor is a comparatively modern lock which replaces two old weirs, one above and one below, whose sites are still marked, the lower by islands and the upper by a footbridge. They have been known by various names which have been much confused one with another, but it would seem that Ark for the lower and Ridge's or Rudge's for the upper one are the most accurate. At Rudge's in the eighteenth century there occurred a fairy-story romance in real life when a certain young nobleman at Oxford fell in love with the weir keeper's daughter Betty and married her in Northmoor Church in 1755. Stranger still to relate, they appear to have lived happily ever after.

At Northmoor Lock we encountered for the first time a worm-and-nut type of gate-paddle gear in place of the customary wheel operated rack. We were informed that the Conservancy were introducing it in place of the latter type, information I find hard to credit. Not only is it very slow to operate, but it is dangerous because it cannot be closed rapidly in the event of a mishap in the lock chamber.

New Bridge, by the mouth of the Windrush, is often described as the oldest extant bridge over the river, perhaps because of the trite paradox thus created. In fact it is not possible to claim the distinction for any one of several bridges with any historical accuracy. On the upper river alone, Radcot Bridge is probably older than New Bridge, and Thacker conjectures that the latter was so called to distinguish it from Radcot rather than from any previous bridge on the same site. New Bridge was built about 1250 and rebuilt by John Golafre in the fifteenth century. With its six pointed arches of grey stone it is a lovely specimen of mediæval bridgework which should stand for many years yet for, happily, traffic on the Abingdon–Witney road which it carries is not very heavy. Consequently, New Bridge seems unlikely to attract the unwelcome attentions of the highway authorities, its width of fifteen feet between parapets being generous for its period.

On each side of the bridge stands a pleasant inn, the 'Maybush' in Berkshire and the 'Rose Revived' on the Oxfordshire bank. The latter was once 'The Rose & Crown' or simply 'The Rose', so that its present title is of comparatively recent origin. But it was a stroke of genius none the less; constituting one of the loveliest and most euphonious of English inn names. The charming original sign of this revival, a single red rose standing in a glass of beer, is now preserved inside the house. Though the old 'Rose' has certainly blossomed out as a hotel, it has equally certainly not become one of those exotic and expensive hybrids such as are all too common on the lower reaches of the river. Moreover, the water traveller is welcomed, and it was a pleasure to patronise the revived 'Rose' in return for the privilege of mooring beside its smooth riverside lawns and massed flowers.

Above New Bridge the Thames becomes a lonely river, avoided by roads and villages for the fear of floods. Except in the height of the summer season it would be possible to travel its course by the hour without meeting a soul other than the lock-keepers or a passer-by at the river crossings at Tadpole or Radcot. Having lost the waters of Evenlode and Windrush, it is a narrow river, so narrow and so winding that our seventy-foot boat had little room to spare on some of the more acute turns.

Shifford, though not actually on the waterside, ventures nearer to the river than any of its neighbours, and its grey stone and thatch is easily visible from the water like that of the adjacent hamlet of Chimney. Both emphasise to the traveller that he is now truly entering the country of that limestone, grey, silver or golden, which first appeared at Abingdon to leaven the brick, timber and tile of the Berkshire vale. Shifford Lock and cut was not opened for traffic until 1898, but we both thought it the most beautiful on the whole length of the Thames. Its large garden, most industriously cultivated by the lock-keeper, admirably combined beauty with utility, and was so fairly set within sheltering trees that the whole resembled a small fertile oasis in the midst of the wide expanse of marsh and watermeadow. It is, in fact, very remote, perhaps the most remote of all Thames stations with the possible exception of Grafton. It is a considerable distance from Shifford village, and in winter it is often isolated by swirling floods. Consequently, the lock-keeper and his family practice self-sufficiency to a remarkable extent. The reward of such independence was reflected in the enthusiasm and pride of the lock-keeper as he showed us his vegetable garden and his livestock, chickens, pigs and goats, all of which he had brought to the lock by boat.

Before Shifford Lock was built there was a series of old navigation weirs on this part of the river: Limbre's Weir under the slopes of Harrowdown Hill, three-quarters of a mile above New Bridge; Shifford, by the mouth of the backwater known as Great Brook and nearer the village than the present lock; Duxford, on the old river channel now by-passed by the Shifford Cut; Tenfoot, so called from the width of its navigation opening, whose site is marked by the footbridge beyond Chimney; Thames Weir, where the river makes a particularly acute turn midway between Tenfoot and Tadpole; and lastly Kent's or Tadpole Weir just below the bridge of that name. Though not on the main river but controlling an outfall, a vanished weir a little above Tadpole deserves mention because of its delightful name of 'Winney Weg's Weir'. With such a succession of weirs to delay navigation, it can be understood how sorely the state of the upper Thames must have prejudiced the fortunes of the Thames & Severn Canal Company so far as through traffic was concerned. We can appreciate the force of the Company's frequent complaints to the Thames Commissioners of delays to their boats. The commendable improvements carried out by the Thames Conservancy came years too late, with the ironical result that the situation is now reversed, an admirable river navigation leading nowhere, and the Thames & Severn fallen into an irretrievable state of dereliction. Such was the fate of what might have become the easiest and best of the old east-to-west water routes.

The traveller emerges from the sheltered length of Shifford Cut on to a broad and treeless tract which the old cartographers would have described as 'Fenny waste'. It is probably the least domesticated bit of country on the whole course of the river, and extends as far as Tenfoot Bridge. Ahead, across these levels, rises the low ridge of hills which here divides the valley of the Thames from the Vale of White Horse, and which marches from Cumner and Fifield by Hinton Waldrist and Buckland to Faringdon. Its most prominent feature from this vantage is the tree-crowned knoll above Faringdon where stands the late Lord Berners' 'Folly' tower. This landmark is seldom or never out of sight of the river all the way to Lechlade.

So modest is the breadth of the river hereabouts that the eighteenth-century bridge at Tadpole consists merely of a single inconsiderable span. Beside it stands the second of the three 'Trout' inns on the upper river. This one once had a landlord by the name of Herring, and its sign then bore the pleasing inscription: "The Trout by A. Herring."

Rushy Lock was opened in 1790 and is remarkable for its handsome lock-house, larger than, and quite different from, the usual design. It stands back from the lock in a large garden which, when we passed through, was ablaze with superb roses.

The explanation is that the house was privately built on private land. The Conservancy owned the lock only and paid the lock-keeper a house allowance to cover rent. In this respect it was the last survival of private ownership in relation to Thames locks and weirs.

In the short and tortuous reach between Rushy and Radcot Locks there were formerly two navigation weirs called Old Nan's and Old Man's, the latter commemorated by the footbridge of that name within sight of Radcot Lock. Here stood yet another weir until the pound-lock was built in 1892. Like so many others on the river, Radcot Weir was privately owned, and Thacker records how the owner put up the tolls on barge traffic following the opening of the Thames & Severn. This short-sighted policy of 'killing the goose' was undoubtedly another of the difficulties which helped to bring that unfortunate canal to ruin.

Radcot Bridge and the nearby Swan Inn are some distance upstream from the lock. Here the line of navigation no longer passes under the old bridge, but follows an artificial cut, constructed in 1787, which is spanned by a single-arch bridge of the same date. Why this cut was ever constructed is not readily apparent. It is narrow and more sharply curved than the old channel, while the bridge is awkwardly placed. The fine old mediæval bridge provides no explanation, because the clearance beneath it is no more restricted than Osney, Godstow or New Bridge. Both Radcot and Newbridge were the scene of skirmishes during the Civil War, when Faringdon held stoutly for the King.

A short reach from Radcot, and above an acute bend called Hell Gut, lies Grafton, another lonely lock, far from the village of that name. It was built in 1896 to replace an old flash weir known variously as Day's, East, New Lock or Lower Hart's.

Beyond Grafton the river prospect tends to become more intimate and domesticated. The lonely levels between Shifford and Radcot have a spaciousness that is almost East Anglian, but here the scale becomes smaller; trees and flood-free slopes draw closer, bringing with them farmsteads and villages; first and most venturesome comes the hamlet of Eaton Hastings on the Berkshire bank, then Kelmscott and finally Buscot. Where the river swings away from Eaton Hastings it is possible to catch a glimpse of the chimneys and clustering gables of Kelmscott Manor behind their screen of sheltering elms (p. 56).

William Morris loved Kelmscott and its neighbourhood. He loved the craftsmanship which, in cottage, barn, manor house or church alike, the grey stone everywhere displayed. He loved, too, the level fields and wide skies which reminded him of his native Essex. In his day, before the invention of the motor car, Kelmscott was indeed remote. It was his 'Nowhere', a land forgotten by that urban civilisation whose works he hated, a land where the ancient partnership of man and nature flowered everywhere in an unselfconscious beauty which seemed to Morris to portend that earthly paradise to which, he believed, an errant world would one day return. Yet it is a paradox that although Morris loved and understood Kelmscott, his dæmonic energy was such that he could never rest there long, whereas his co-tenant Rossetti,

66

Rossetti the sensuous, drug-haunted urban intellectual who had no genuine feeling whatever for the English countryside, lingered on at Kelmscott from sheer indolence and a liking for Janey which was, perhaps, less than discreet. While Morris the ever-restless embarked for Iceland in search of a world even more remote, Rossetti filled Kelmscott with friends as incongruous in such surroundings as himself, or wrote long letters in which he complained of the house, its 'deadly flat' surroundings and the 'one-eyed' character of the neighbouring town of Lechlade. Morris himself said of Rossetti that: "He has all sorts of ways so unsympathetic with the sweet simple old place that I feel his presence there a kind of slur on it", and it was a relief to him when Rossetti finally left, ostensibly as a result of a quarrel with some fishermen on the river.

It is fitting that it is Morris's name, not Rossetti's, which will always be linked with Kelmscott, for although his temperament did not allow him to lead the bucolic life of a countryman *adscriptus glebæ*, no man of his generation appreciated so clearly the merit of that way of life of which the gracious stonework of his manor house was so eloquent an affirmation. Moreover, this tempestuous genius returned at the last to Kelmscott to lie in the graveyard of the little Early English church of St. George. One October day in 1896 when the skies wept for him and the Thames had invaded the meadows in sudden autumn flood, Morris was borne thither on his last journey in a Cotswold waggon resplendent in its traditional ochre and scarlet, and decorated with sprigs of vine and willow boughs.

Kelmscott Manor was tenantless at the time we visited it. Within the seclusion of its walled garden the old house basked in the hot June sunlight, as silent, as lovely and as serene as on the day when Topsy, Janey and Dante Gabriel, drawn thither by a house agent's advertisement, set eyes on it for the first time. Thanks to the kindness of the present lease-holder, we were able to pass through the magic door in the wall and see over the house. It was a fascinating experience, but a salutary one for any devotee of the Pre-Raphaelites. The garden had become a wilderness. By comparison with the living, timeless quality of craftsmanship which the fabric of the house reflected, the relics of Pre-Raphaelite occupation appeared unbelievably pathetic, when one recalled the high enthusiasm and aspirations of the Brotherhood. Stylised, dated and dead they seemed; the bric-à-brac of a highly self-conscious experiment which could never achieve the immortal stature of true greatness, because it sought to escape from rather than to transcend the problems of the contemporary world. Perhaps the best Pre-Raphaelite memorials at Kelmscott are the Morris wallpapers, though even these seem somewhat inappropriate in small, low-ceilinged and rather dark rooms. Much more inappropriate is the tapestry which completely envelops the small upstairs sitting-room from floor to ceiling, doors included. The effect here is monstrous. An occupant of the room feels completely hemmed in by writhing figures, larger than life-size, which enact the story of Samson, including a nightmarish scene in which that unfortunate worthy is about to have his eyes gouged out. This tapestry went with the house when Morris and Rossetti acquired it, but the fact that they never removed it, to make what would otherwise be a delightful room, is a curious comment upon Pre-Raphaelite taste. It is true that Rossetti reviled the tapestry in his letters, but for some reason he lacked the courage to remove it. Could Topsy have objected? However that may be, Rossetti achieved the highly unsatisfactory compromise of hanging his pictures on top of it. The agonised Samson does not make the happiest of room-mates for Dante Gabriel's long-necked and languishing damosels.

Kelmscott might be as lovely inside as out if the Pre-Raphaelite relics could be assembled in one room for the benefit of pilgrims, and the rest of the house was allowed to forget its illustrious occupants whose tenancy was, after all, but a brief interlude in its long history. Could he return, William Morris would, I am sure, be the first to agree. Like all great artists and craftsmen his thoughts and aspirations moved always ahead of his practical achievements.

Within sight of Kelmscott the 'Anchor' inn stands close beside the river at the point where the north bank passes from Oxfordshire into Gloucestershire. This inn, with its accompanying footbridge, marks the site of Eaton Weir, the last flash weir of the old paddle-and-rimer type to survive on the Thames. Thacker in his *Thames Highway* includes a photograph of the weir taken in 1910 which shows the paddles drawn and a punt passing through the opening. As at Medley, the river now makes a level at Eaton.

After passing the site of Eaton Weir the balance beams of Buscot Lock soon come into view across the meadows, but it takes some time to reach the lock, so persistently and acutely does the river wind. Buscot, opened in 1790, is the only unattended lock on the Thames, while its weir was the last survival of the once common practice of private ownership, being the property of Buscot Park. The lock keeper of St. John's is responsible for Buscot, with the result that the crews of craft bound upstream should be prepared to work the lock themselves.

Above Buscot Lock the Georgian rectory of Buscot and the church with its barrel ceiling and Burne Jones window stand close beside the little river, which here again winds most deviously on its way to St. John's, the first, or last, and the highest lock on the Thames (p. 50). Like Buscot Lock, it was built in 1790 following the completion of the Thames & Severn Canal. Beside it the ancient bridge of St. John crosses the weir stream. It was built originally in the thirteenth century and was maintained by the monks of the Priory of St. John which adjoined it. The Priory disappeared long before the dissolution, and much of its stone was used in rebuilding Lechlade Church, to which St. John's is linked by a causeway over the meadows. But tradition asserts that part of the monastic buildings are incorporated in the old inn which now stands by the bridge-foot and which was formerly called 'St. John the Baptist's Head'. It has now become yet another Thames-side 'Trout', but apart from its name it can have changed very little within memory. We have advanced beyond the furthest perimeter of that commercial exploitation of the river which attempts to combine the 'old world' and the new with such shocking and expensive results. Here is still the authentic riverside inn wherein bargemen and fishermen long dead would even now feel at home and at ease. Its bar has an extremely low ceiling, and as its floor is well below the present road level, its small windows shed little light upon an interior yellowed and fogged by the smoke of strong tobacco. An effect of sub-aqueous gloom is enhanced by the glassy stare of the monster fish, ranged in their cases along the walls to encourage the efforts of successive generations of anglers. The whole is the antithesis of modern ideas of architecture and interior decoration, but faithfully reflects the preference of an older generation of country-men who spent their long working days in the open air and, when they were done, demanded cosiness, not scientific hygiene. This venerable establishment is presided over by a landlord who can almost certainly boast a longer record of continuous tenancy than any other Thames-side innkeeper.

The quiet meadows below the bridge where the little River Leach joins the Thames were once the scene of much activity. Here there was a great five-day fair, founded, no doubt at the instance of the Priory, in 1234 on the Feast of the Decolla-tion. Here also there were busy wharves until the coming of the canal to Inglesham, and the Baskerville MS. describes both as follows:—

"St. John Bridge fair is kept on the 29 day of August in the Meadow below ye bridge on Glocester shire side, to wch Oxford boats & others resort to sell Ale, Beef & Carrots, & to carry goods from this fair down stream. And here at a Mill below this Meadow, Leach flu runs into Tems, which stream I suppose divides Glocester shier from Oxford shier. Many boats come hither to lade & unlade goods, I have seen 6 or 8 boats togeither at their Wharfe. Ffor besides Corn of all sorts wch they lade to go down stream, here comes from Severn and Avon landed at Tewsbery where both these rivers do unite and elswere, on horses and in Carts & Wagons by land great weights of Cheese especially that sort goes by y name of Cheshire Cheese, for hereabout The Boates Masters have warehouses to secure their goods; And Hoys in time of scarcity, & other goods comes from London-ward hether & are sent as aforesaid by land to Severn and thence in Boats to Bristol and elswere, & in ships to Ireland."

There is considerable doubt about the western navigable limit of the Thames in the days before the coming of the canal. Thacker conjectures, and puts forward evidence to support his theory that, incredible though it may seem today, Ashton Keynes once boasted a wharf at Waterhay Bridge, over four miles west of Cricklade. Certainly the river was once navigated to Cricklade, and this was generally regarded as the western head of the navigation by the seventeenth-century Oxford–Burcot Commission and by all subsequent authorities, a circumstance acknowledged to this day by the fact that the town forms the limit of the jurisdiction of the Thames Conservancy. Westhall, writing in 1828, long after the canal was built, records that barges of only six or seven tons burden could navigate to West Mill Cricklade, and it seems obvious that while there may once have been local trade to and from that town in craft of small capacity, the wharf at St. John's, and another directly below the school at Lechlade, constituted between them the western terminal of the Thames barge traffic. The quotation from Baskerville virtually proves this, for, at the time of which he wrote, river navigation, for all its delays and hazards, was so much cheaper than overland carriage that Cricklade would undoubtedly have become the point of transhipment for the Severn in preference to St. John's had this been practicable.

Just above St. John's the little River Cole flows into the Thames from the neighbourhood of Swindon. For the greater part of its course it forms the Wiltshire county boundary, and it thus marks the end of Berkshire's monopoly of the south bank of the Thames, which extends all the way to Runnymede. The Cole also calls attention to the remarkable absence of tributaries on this bank of the Thames west of the Kennet at Reading. On the north there are Thame, Cherwell, Evenlode, Windrush, Leach, Coln and Churn, but on the south the only other noteworthy contributions to the river are the Ock, at Abingdon, and the little River Ray which enters below Cricklade.

Like the 'Trout' at St. John's, Lechlade has remained true to its traditional character and purpose. It has not curried the favours of the industrialist nor has it prostituted itself as a 'beauty spot'. Though buses convey too many of its inhabitants to work in the factories of Swindon, Lechlade still endeavours, so far as it is able in our topsy-turvy and ill-balanced world, to perform the ancient functions of the small country town. Small it certainly is, being indeed little more than a large village, but with its comely houses of cool grey stone, and its wide square and streets, it possesses the same airy, spacious dignity which characterises the Wold towns of Burford, Stow, Northleach or Campden. So perfectly does Lechlade express their idiom that it might indeed stand in the heart of the Wolds instead of upon their borders at only 230 feet above sea level. Only rarely, as in the brickwork of the New Inn, does the town acknowledge the fact that just across the river lies the Vale of White Horse. The Thames virtually forms the southern boundary of stone building between Oxford and Cricklade. Stone buildings there may be south of the river, but they are no more than outposts in a territory of brick, timber, tile and thatch or, as the downs draw near, flint.

We arrived at Lechlade on midsummer day and, so far as our boat was concerned, this was journey's end. We moored by the willow-fringed edge of the meadow which here divides town from river, a meadow dominated by Lechlade's lovely spire of Taynton stone, that same 'dim and distant spire' which, in some summer's dusk so long ago, inspired Shelley's poem. Here we stayed while the hay in the meadow was cut and turned and carried, while red roses budded, bloomed and faded against the grey walls of Church House, and the church clock counted away the hours and days. Reverberating in the still air of the scented fields, this clock bell seemed with sweet but sad insistence to sing the transcience of things, to be sounding away, not the hours of mortal reckoning but falling roses, the fading summer grasses and life itself.

70

28   A Bridge on the Upper Thames, possibly St. John's, Lechlade, 1825, before rebuilding

From a watercolour by George Shepherd

In the Ashmolean Museum, Oxford

A hundred yards or so above our mooring, Halfpenny Bridge crossed the river in a single lofty span. As its name indicates, it was once a toll bridge and its little toll house still stands beside it. Like the locks at Buscot and St. John's, the bridge and its causeway over the flood-meadows to the south was an improvement coincident with the coming of the canal to Inglesham. Before it was built there was a ferry and ford only at this point. The old road to the south was the by-way known as Barkers Lane, which leaves the Faringdon road at Buscot, beyond St. John's Bridge, crosses the Cole at Lynt Bridge, and joins the present road near the hamlet of Inglesham. When the canal was opened, new wharves were built at Lechlade just above the bridge, and the old wharves below the school and at St. John's went out of use. The buildings of these later wharves still exist, though they have been turned to other uses.

Across the meadows from Halfpenny Bridge can be seen the distinctive round tower lock-house of stone which marks the entrance of the Thames & Severn Canal. It is the first of many similar towers which stand sentinel beside this lost and derelict waterway as it marches over the wolds and down the Golden Valley to Brimscombe. It was to Inglesham that Shelley came with his Mary, having rowed by easy stages all the way from Old Windsor with the object of reaching Thames Head. Shelley planned to use the canal to attain this objective and then to continue westwards to the Severn. But the Canal Company, it is said, demanded £20 toll for the through journey, an exorbitant sum which the poet would not pay. They accordingly continued up the river, but were eventually defeated by weed and lack of water, and never got to Thames Head.

We also rowed up the river from Lechlade one bright afternoon, but without the ambitions of our most illustrious forerunner. This meeting-place of waterways is of a beauty made melancholy by the death of the old canal which once brought so much life to the upper Thames. Long green tresses of water-weed wave in the waters of the idle Thames, and fat trout bask in the clear pools of the Coln, which flows in just below the canal entrance, where a graceful wooden bridge carries the towpath over the river. In a setting of spiring poplars, the round tower and the grey stone house beside it contemplate the derelict canal lock and the little bridge at its tail. Carved on the keystone of this bridge is an inscription which proudly records that the junction of canal and river was effected on November 14th 1789. Five days later the first barge from the Severn, with a flag flying at her masthead, sailed bravely down the river to Lechlade and St. John's, to be greeted by a cheering crowd and a salute of cannon from Buscot Park. What junketings there were then! The ringing of bells; a special dinner at the five principal inns of Lechlade; a bonfire and a grand ball. It is all forgotten now. The empty lock chamber is almost lost in a tangle of climbing roses; gates and beams have rotted away, though one still hangs intact. It swung easily when I leant against its beam, though it groaned in its quoins as though to protest against me for disturbing so long and sound a sleep. Beyond the lock the canal bed has become a head-high jungle of reeds and undergrowth. Yet we managed to follow its course as far as the curious and even more overgrown double lock by Dudgrove Farm, where they still remember consigning their Gloster cheeses by water.

Rowing on up the river, we landed once more to visit the little church of Inglesham, which stands close beside the bank upon a low mound. Unlike many of our visits to Thames-side churches, this one was rewarding indeed. The country church, ideally, should exemplify the work of each successive generation. The heterogeneous result may distress the purists and the tidy-minded, but a church is not merely a piece of architecture to be judged solely by æsthetic standards as the monument of a particular age. Rather should it be regarded as a symbol of immanence, a witness of eternal verities transcending the temporal. Continuity is essentially the manifestation of this supernatural significance, a continuity expressed by the hand of the craftsman sharing with his predecessors a common purpose which reduces to order an apparent disorder. At Inglesham, in a building little larger than a cottage, there survives to a unique degree this sense of continuity. Each century has made its contribution in its own way, and yet the affirmation of each unifies the whole. In the wall there is set a Madonna and Child of the eleventh century; part of the fabric dates from the twelfth century; there is a thirteenth-century triple Sedilia and two splendid oak screens, one of the fourteenth and the other of the fifteenth century; there are Carolean pews in the chancel and high eighteenth-century box pews in the nave. Finally, some Thames-side craftsman has made one of the simplest but most fitting contributions by covering the hassocks in woven river rushes.

In the late nineteenth century, Inglesham Church fell into disrepair. The fate it might have suffered if the ardent Victorian restorer had fallen upon it can be easily visualised, for examples of his handiwork are all too common along the course of the Thames. He would have torn out the old pews and replaced the uneven flags of the floor by neat, brightly-coloured encaustic tiles. The screens would have had to go, too, because they would have broken the serried ranks of new pitch-pine pews. The walls, of course, would have to be stripped and heavily repointed. . . . Happily its remoteness saved Inglesham from such a fate, until there came to its rescue the only man in the England of that day who understood and respected the continuity of craftsmanship to which it bears such eloquent testimony. A small wall tablet records that:—

'This church was repaired in 1888-9 through
the energy and with the help of
William Morris
who loved it.'

There is no finer memorial to Topsy than this little church upon which his hand rested so lightly and so lovingly.

Immediately above this tablet commemorating Morris's help is an eighteenth-century memorial to a certain John Matthews of Lynt and his wife Elizabeth. The last lines caught my eye. They read:—

'Life how short!
Eternity how long!'

They might well, I thought, have been the motto of William Morris, who lived his life with such eager and tempestuous energy. But they are also the text of the sermon preached by each stick and stone of the church that he loved.

From Inglesham the Thames winds on its lonely way through the fields by the grey villages of Kempsford and Castle Eaton to Cricklade. Venturesome hirers of rowing boats from Lechlade sometimes row beyond Inglesham, but soon the little river is left alone with no company but the cows, staring down from the banks at their reflections or wading into the shallows.

The churches of Kempsford and Castle Eaton both stand close to the river. Both are worth visiting, though they have suffered the fate which might so easily have befallen Inglesham. Kempsford is a church of remarkable size and noble proportions. Within, there is a beautiful lofty lantern of painted stonework beneath the tower, Norman windows and doorways in the nave and a sermon glass in a bracket beside the pulpit. But, alas, the Victorians have left their mark in the shape of painted texts on the walls, execrable glass and a south chapel of peculiar hideousness. They have been less unkind to the smaller church at Castle Eaton, which has a curious little thirteenth-century bell turret with a conical cap like a witch's hat. Its bell was removed to the fifteenth-century tower, but has been happily restored to it. Just above the churchyard is Castle Eaton Bridge, an unedifying iron structure erected in 1893 to replace the old bridge of timber on stone piers.

At Cricklade the Thames loses the waters of the rivers Ray and Churn to become a stream of so modest a size as scarcely to justify the name of river. Beyond the town the derelict North Wilts Canal crosses over the river on its course from the Wilts & Berks at Swindon to the Thames & Severn at Latton. It treats the Thames with scant respect, relegating it to a series of culverts beneath its embankment. There are some who argue, indeed, that this stream should not be called the Thames at all, but that either the Coln or the Churn in fact constitute the upper river. In my view, however, to see the confluence of these two streams at Inglesham and Cricklade is to be left in no doubt at all as to which is the parent river and which the tributary. The claim of the stream which rises at Thames Head cannot be seriously disputed.

Cricklade, like Lechlade, has a wide and spacious main street, but it carries the heavy traffic of Ermine Street and so lacks the quiet of Lechlade, where traffic is never dense even in the height of summer. It was very unkind of Cobbett to call Cricklade a 'villainous hole', although I must confess that it has always struck me as a rather bleak and mean little town. There is much stone building, but it seems to lack the dignity of Lechlade, a true Cotswold town, and to belong, despite its stone, almost

73

wholly to the Vale. It is a pleasant fancy to suppose that this allegiance is due to its situation on the south bank of the Thames.

The large, handsome church of St. Sampson's, Cricklade, reflects, as do many Cotswold churches, the lost prosperity of the age of the 'golden fleece'. Its great Late Perpendicular tower is the lighthouse of this part of the vale, although, with it unduly massive turrets and pinnacles and its blank tracery, it is a rather cumbersome piece of work with little of the grace of the other wool churches. Its lofty interior lantern, however, is magnificent and bears within it the heraldic devices of its sixteenth-century patrons: the silver saltire, red rose and bear and staff of Warwick; the chequy banner and the crescent badge of Northumberland. There are also four curious emblems resembling the four suits of playing-cards, the significance of which never seems to have been convincingly explained.

A little over four miles by water from Cricklade, and a short distance upstream from Waterhay Bridge, the Swill Brook enters the Thames. Above the confluence of this, its first tributary, the river becomes a mere brook. Whether or no Thacker is correct in his supposition that there was once a wharf at Waterhay, it is quite certain that no craft of even the smallest commercial burden could ever have proceeded any further upstream. Was nearby Ashton Keynes ever the head of the Thames Navigation? It is a large straggling village set about a maze of intersecting lanes which certainly suggests that it was once a place of much greater importance. Beside the length of its main street babbles the little Thames, spanned by a succession of small bridges which give access to the grey houses with their bright gardens which flank its opposite bank. At the head of this northward-facing street the stream turns sharply westwards. Here its waters are seen to emerge from a culvert and to be surrounded thus upon three sides by old cottages and gardens, while away to the right a footpath leads to the church through a great avenue of elms. Like Arlington Row at Bibury, this little corner looks almost too good to be true, and one expects to find amateur watercolourists busily at work. But it seems to be little known and frequented, and on the occasion of our visit it was drowsing very peacefully in the warm sunlight of the high summer afternoon. There is something dramatic in the way that the Thames emerges from its culvert into the midst of this attractive picture, so that one feels that this should properly be regarded as its source. But in fact its waters have already travelled, in theory at any rate, six miles. Already it has passed the stone villages of Ewen and Somerford Keynes on its way from its source near the Roman Fosse Way.

Above Kempsford the river ceases to form a county boundary and is wholly in Wiltshire, but west of Ashton Keynes it crosses the border of that county, and so it is Gloucestershire which gives birth to the Thames. It is not a dramatic birth, in fact the precise place of birth varies with weather and season. Officially its source is marked by an ash tree, bearing the letters T. H. carved upon its trunk, which stands in Trewsbury Mead west of the Fosse Way. A culvert is provided to carry its waters under the road, yet in fact it is but rarely that water is to be found thus far. More commonly the floor of the valley must be followed on the east side of the road until the first little runnel of water appears. It will usually be found near the site of the old Thames Head pumping station, whose foundations can still be seen, which once filled with water the dry bed of the old canal that winds along the contours of the valley on its way to the mouth of the great tunnel in Hailey wood.

Here on these rolling, windy wolds is the watershed, the farthest reach of Thames. Only a few miles further westward, over the wooded skyline of the Cotswold scarp, the Frome and its tributaries hurry down their steep valleys to the Severn sea. But this tiny silver stream is destined upon a longer and more momentous journey before it can lose itself in the tossing seas beyond the Nore. It must travel the length of a land that has had more influence upon human destiny than any other, the most famous river valley in the whole world.

The Thames Head Pumping Station in 1878
From a drawing by Samuel Owen

75

NOTES ON THE ILLUSTRATIONS

Frontispiece 1 Eton College and Chapel from the River

By W. Westall, A.R.A. Engraved by R. G. Reeves, circa 1828

It is perhaps not unfitting that the frontispiece should be devoted to a view of Eton, with its five centuries of memories and associations with English life and eminent men, and where, as Percy Lubbock wrote, "The River throws its arm about Eton with an ample swing". Many old buildings remain in its complex structure since the foundation by Henry VI in 1440, but from the river little is seen except a range of Georgian Gothic recalling many Cambridge colleges, backed by the splendid spacious Perpendicular chapel paralleling that of King's College, Cambridge, and built about the same time for the same royal saint. Its outstanding murals of the miracles of the Virgin have, after brutal treatment, been recently revealed and restored.

2 Gravesend from the Thames

By S. Owen. Engraved by R. G. Reeves, circa 1828

Gravesend is still the gateway to the Port of London, where incoming ships are quickly and efficiently passed for health and Customs. The town, which has some old streets with weatherboarded houses, was largely rebuilt after a severe fire in 1727; St. George's parish church, plain Georgian, dates from 1731–3, and still survives. It is the burying place of Pocahontas and has a fine candelabrum. Windmill Hill, now a recreation ground, commands superb views of the endless pageant of shipping. Though Gravesend does not cater largely for visitors, Londoners used to holiday there in 1828, when it was proud of its seven bathing-machines.

3 Tilbury Fort

By S. Owen. Engraved by R. G. Reeves, circa 1828

The Tilbury of 1828 consisted of the fort and a few scattered houses; now the great docks, commenced in 1882, cover more than a square mile, and the floating landing stage is nearly a quarter of a mile long. The white Baroque water-gate is carved with trophies and dates from 1682. It is curious that the schooner-rigged paddle steamer *Venus* flies the white ensign.

4 Greenwich Hospital from the River

By S. Owen. Engraved by R. G. Reeves, circa 1828

The Hospital, or Royal Naval College, is well seen here. The greatest of English Late Renaissance buildings, it achieves a noble and dignified unity in spite of its composite design and construction in several stages between 1662 and 1752, with contributions by John Webb, Wren, Hawksmoor, Vanbrugh, Colin Campbell and Ripley. Inigo Jones' Queen's House (*circa* 1616), the focal point, is seen behind, between the domes, and on the hill the buildings of the Observatory, which now functions from Hurstmonceux Castle, Sussex.

5   Greenwich Hospital from the Park Hill looking towards London

By John Dobbin, signed and dated 1851

This view, painted in the year of the Great Exhibition, is one which was a particular favourite among artists and engravers of the eighteenth century, who recorded it in a number of versions. Inigo Jones's Queen's House is seen in front of the two domes, with the chapel on the left. The buildings of Flamsteed's Observatory, before later alterations, appear on the left. The Park deer, with well developed antlers, seem as tame as they are abundant.

6   The Thames at Deptford

By Samuel Scott, circa 1760

These pleasant weatherboarded dwellings, with good chimneys and red-tiled roofs, have long disappeared. It is surprising that no other buildings are in sight. On the platform at the top of the steps above the foreshore is a curious wooden erection, possibly a kind of crane.

7   The Castle and River Medway, Tonbridge, Kent, 1795

By J. Farington, R.A. Engraved by J. C. Stadler

This scene, selected to show the Thames' chief eastern tributary, is delightful in Farington's grouping, with the plain but dignified classic bridge connecting two irregular but pleasant batches of old houses, the placid river and the ruined castle on its wooded mound. Its importance as a crossing has led to its complete modernisation.

8   The Tower of London in 1795

By J. Farington, R.A. Engraved by J. C. Stadler

The Tower of London, "probably the most valuable monument of mediæval military architecture remaining in this country", has been at times a fortress, a political prison and a royal palace. A comparison with a modern view shows that practically all the irregular later buildings huddled round the great central Keep, the White Tower, built in 1078 by Gundulph, Bishop of Rochester, have been swept away by Victorian restorations, which if in some ways regrettable, have brought back more of the outer aspect of a mediæval fortress. Note the two rowing boats towing upstream the sailing ship with its huge bowsprit.

9   The Custom House and Shipping in the Upper Pool

By S. Owen. Engraved by R. G. Owen, circa 1828

Here is a varied and attractive crowd of sailing shipping, with the smacks clustering thickly round Billingsgate, and the Dutch eel boats off the Custom House, from which they have only lately been banished. All are now replaced by Europe-trading steamers of fair size. Laing's Custom House, with its famous Long Room, dates from 1817, but the centre was expensively reconstructed to Smirke's designs in 1825. The Monument, St. Paul's and St. Magnus, now, as then, rise in the background.

10   New London Bridge opened 1831

By G. Yates, 1830

This view of new London Bridge from the west is taken in 1830, the year before its opening, when it was practically finished from the designs of John Rennie, completed by his son. Through the arches it is interesting to see the last stage of the old bridge a little to the east, still in use before it was cleared away after an existence of over six centuries.

77

11   Old London Bridge, demolished 1757

By T. M. Baynes, 1824

This view of Old London Bridge from the east enables us to recall the irregular jumbled ranges of shops and houses removed in 1757, and the close-set piers and "starlings" which were so dangerous an impediment to navigation. The detail can be finely seen in Hollar's view of the late seventeenth century, which includes an assortment of traitors' heads on spikes. There is also a fine model in the London Museum.

12   An Eighteenth-Century View of the Thames looking East
from the Gardens of Old Somerset House

By Antonio Canaletto

The charming terrace gardens of Old Somerset House afforded other artists than Canaletto, such as Paul Sandby, a vantage point from which to depict the Thames, down and up. From it is seen the broad sweep of the river, the red brick warehouses lining the north bank, surmounted by the great dome of St Paul's, which contrasts with the numerous slender steeples of Wren's churches pricking the sky. How small a proportion remains to be visible to future generations!

13   A Boatbuilding Yard and Workshops at Battersea

By Samuel Scott, circa 1760

These buildings compare with, but differ from, those at Deptford by the same artist (Figure 6), but are equally admirable. The large gabled shed with its piles of timber was probably for boat-building; it is suggested that the kiln, with possibly a furnace lower down, was the Battersea enamel factory. The distance with its windmills is reminiscent of Holland. All this has now been swept away.

14   Richmond by the Bridge

By Thomas Hearne, 1790

Hearne's watercolour shows Richmond wooded to the top of the hill, with its famous and still lovely view, and the reverse of over-built. Today its narrow streets are bustling and queue-crowded, but fortunately the graceful bridge of 1777, designed by James Paine the architect, though widened, still spans the river, and there are excellent Georgian houses and terraces dotted about, so that much of its attractive historical character remains.

15   A Distant View of Windsor Castle

By John Glover

20   Windsor Castle from Cooper's Hill, 1798

By J. Farington, R.A. Engraved by J. C. Stadler

These two pictures, while affording an interesting comparison and contrast in colouring and technique by the individual artists, agree in their effective representation of the rolling, thickly wooded country of parks and chases south of Windsor. Glover's view (Figure 15) looks north and slightly east; Farington's faces the north-west, with the Thames on the right. In both, the distant range of the Castle is shown before its Gothicising transmogrification by Wyatville in 1824.

16 Kingston-on-Thames, Surrey, 1818

By George Shepherd

The Royal Borough of Kingston-on-Thames has, unlike its neighbour Richmond, retained little of its historic character, with only a few old houses among many imposing modern buildings. The simple old timber bridge, of a type frequently met with over a century ago on the Thames, was replaced by a stone structure in 1828. The massive brick tower of the church dates from 1703, and still remains; the Gothic building itself has been heavily restored. Kingston is the terminus of the Oxford steamers.

17 The Church and City Stone, Staines, Middlesex

From an aquatint by Robert Havell, 1811

Havell shows that the old Stone was set in delightful surroundings 140 years ago; it is now in a recreation ground, with a gasworks on the Surrey bank. The Stone, raised on a plinth, is inscribed "God preserve ye City of London", and on its base "Conservators of the River Thames". It formerly marked the western limit of the City of London's control of the river, and is still on the Middlesex–Buckinghamshire border. The church tower dates from 1631, but has been re-topped; the rest was rebuilt in 1828.

18 Datchet Ferry, near Windsor, Berkshire

From an aquatint by Robert Havell, 1811

It is well that Havell has recorded a typical Thames cart ferry, by the tall Restoration house. The old Queen Anne bridge had been reduced to grass-topped piers, and a year later than this view, in 1812, the counties of Buckinghamshire and Berkshire, after quarrelsome exchanges, built a composite affair of wood and iron, joined at the middle arch. Wombwell's circus elephant-van fell through this piece of tinkering one day, and the bridge was replaced in 1851 by the twin Victoria-and-Albert iron structures a mile and a half up and down the stream. The ferry no longer exists.

19 Windsor Castle and the Thames at Windsor, Berkshire

From a print of 1865

This view of the Castle across the river shows its whole length; to the left is seen the immense range of the neo-Gothic turrets and walls set up by Wyatville between 1824 and 1840; in the first six years £500,000 was expended. He was also responsible for raising the Round Tower to twice its original height. To the right is St George's chapel, its Perpendicular mercifully untouched, a gem of English late Gothic ranking with the chapels of King's College, Cambridge, of Henry VII, Westminster, and of Eton. On the right edge is the Clewer Tower with Salvin's incongruous cap. The little train is amusing.

20 Windsor Castle and Bridge, 1798 (*v. page 78*)

21 The Thames near Fawley Court, Henley, Oxfordshire

From an aquatint by Robert Havell, 1811

This spot is at the end of Henley Reach, two miles below the town. The river sweeps in a broad curve round to Hambleden Mill, and to the north the wooded Chilterns rise past several estates to the remote hamlet of Fawley. It is scenically one of the finest places on the upper Thames, and may rank with Day's Lock under the Wittenham Clumps, Streatley Hill, and Hart's Woods above Pangbourne. The C.P.R.E. Thames Report recommends the protecting preservation of this stretch.

22   Henley-on-Thames, Oxfordshire, 1818

By George Shepherd

One is inclined to think the bright little Georgian town is at its pleasantest in its normal workaday guise, and not in its hectic regatta fever. It is difficult to say which is the most attractive of Henley, Marlow and Abingdon on the upper river; all have great charm, and individual preference may decide. The scene in this north-looking view is largely unchanged today; the graceful bridge of 1786 is flanked by the bay-windowed 'Angel' inn (there is another 'Angel' on the Berkshire side) and the large red-brick 'Red Lion'. St. Mary's Church with its flint chequerwork is spacious but rather cold Perpendicular; its fine tower has lost its spirelet.

23   St. Peter's Church with Castle in the Background, Wallingford, Berkshire

From an aquatint by Robert Havell, 1811

Wallingford is another pleasant little place; its river crossing was always of great importance, and in Norman times the town had three monasteries and fourteen churches; now there are but three. Havell's view shows the bridge under reconstruction—with water being pumped out of a caisson and a temporary wooden affair; St. Peter's church before it was rebuilt by Sir Robert Taylor with an open octagonal steeple; and considerable remains of the great Norman Castle, of which only some scraps of stonework and the huge motte are extant. Much of the town's earthern ramparts remain on the west.

24,   Abingdon, Berkshire, *circa* 1820

By George Shepherd

25   The Bridge and Church at Abingdon, Berkshire

From an aquatint by Robert Havell, 1811

The two views of Abingdon present an interesting difference in interpretation, though taken from but a slight difference in position and a few years in time. Abingdon is one of the most delightful old towns in England, as writers have for three centuries borne witness. It is full of streets of characterful old houses, but does not photograph easily. The group of St. Helen's spired five-aisled church with its ranges of almshouses is unequalled. To the right of Shepherd's view is seen the outline of Kempster's County Hall, 1678–83, and below are the buildings which incorporate the scanty domestic remains of its great vanished Abbey. Some of the mediæval bridge remains after the partial rebuilding in 1928.

26   Oxford from Wytham Hill

By William Turner 'of Oxford'

It is fitting that this view of Oxford city should be by the local artist, William Turner 'of Oxford', most of whose working life was passed within its boundaries. It is taken from the 500–600-feet wooded slopes of the coral rag ridge of Wytham Hill, and looking eastward the towers and spires of the city are seen from north to south, with the westerly Thames stream on its way down from Godstow.

27   Witney and Coggs, and the River Windrush, Oxfordshire, *circa* 1820

By George Shepherd

As the Medway at Tonbridge represents an eastern tributary (Figure 6), so Figure 27, the Windrush at Witney, may stand for the principal western affluent, and also show a typical old Cotswold town.

Witney has devoted itself to the manufacture of blankets for centuries, and the building of large modern factories has luckily left it most of its attractive traditional appearance. The stately cruciform church, thirteenth to fifteenth centuries, with a typical Oxfordshire pinnacled broach spire, stands apart across a wide green. To the left is the little adjoining hamlet of Coggs, with its octagonal tower detached from the church.

28   A Bridge on the Upper Thames, possibly St. John's, Lechlade, 1825

By George Shepherd

This drawing by Shepherd represents a typical scene in the river's highest reaches, where the modest stream flows between flat well-wooded clay meadows, yet it has over 200 feet to drop before it reaches the sea. Though the crossing is of importance, the scene is entirely peaceful, and it is not easy to realise how these places were the scenes of sudden fierce, if brief, skirmishes during the years of the Civil War.

NOTES ON THE ARTISTS REPRESENTED

For titles of the subjects represented, vide the descriptive list of illustrations preceding these notes.

Figures 1, 2, 3, 4 and 9 have been reproduced from *Picturesque Tour of the River Thames,* by W. Westall, A.R.A., published by Ackermann in 1828. R. G. Reeves engraved in aquatint all the 24 illustrations "from original drawings taken on the spot" by William Westall, A.R.A. (1781–1850) and Samuel Owen (1768 or 1769–1857). Westall was born in Hertford and became an A.R.A. in 1812. He worked principally as a topographical artist, not only in England but in Australia, China, India, Madeira and the West Indies as well. Samuel Owen is known mainly as a marine artist; he exhibited at the Academy from 1794–1807.

Figure 5 is from a watercolour by John Dobbin, a Londoner, and a topographical painter flourishing during the period 1842–1884. He exhibited frequently at the Royal Academy during those years, at the British Institution and at the Society of British Artists, and also painted landscape subjects in Scotland, France and Spain as well as in England. He worked in oil and watercolour, and two of his views were lithographed for J. P. Lawson's *Scotland Delineated,* 1847–54.

Figures 6 and 13 are from watercolours by Samuel Scott (1710?–1772), known for his many paintings of London and the Thames. He was much influenced by Canaletto, and indeed became known as "the English Canaletto". His work was much admired by Horace Walpole, whose collection contained several paintings by him.

Figures 7, 8 and 20 have been reproduced from Boydell's *History of the River Thames,* 1794–96. J. C. Stadler engraved the 64 aquatint plates from original drawings by Joseph Farington, R.A. Farington (1747–1821) was born at Leigh in Lancashire. He was one of the first students at the Academy, of which he became an Associate in 1783 and an R.A. two years later. Farington is known also as the author of an extensive *Diary* which is informative, particularly about contemporary artists. J. C. Stadler was a German engraver who worked from 1780 to 1812 in London, and engraved views in aquatint.

81

Figure 12, from the Royal Collection, is by Antonio Canal, or Canaletto as he is commonly known. Born in Venice in 1697 and dying there in 1768, he is principally famous for the immense series of views of his native city. In 1746 Canaletto visited London and remained for two years, painting there many of his finest pictures of scenes of London and the Thames. The painting here reproduced is thought to have been executed after his return to Venice, and to have been commissioned by the English Consul, Smith.

Thomas Hearne (1744–1817) painted the watercolour shown in Figure 14 in 1790. It is signed and dated in the bottom left-hand corner. Hearne was born at Brinkworth, near Malmesbury, and came to London when very young. His life was spent as a topographical draughtsman, principally of English scenes, but also, for a short period, of the Leeward Islands, when in 1771 he was appointed draughtsman to the Governor.

Figure 15. Distant view of Windsor Castle, is by John Glover (1767–1849). He was born at Houghton-on-the-Hill, Leicestershire, came to London in 1805, and in 1830 or 1831 he departed for Tasmania, where he passed the remainder of his life. He worked both in oil and watercolour, and exhibited at the Royal Academy, the Old Water Colour Society, and the Society of British Artists, which he helped to found.

George Sidney Shepherd was a watercolour painter who exhibited topographical scenes at the Royal Academy and elsewhere from 1800 to 1830. Figures 16, 22, 24, 27 and 28 form part of a series which he was commissioned to paint as extra illustrations to a pair of the most richly 'Grangerized' books of all time: a copy of Clarendon's *History of the Great Rebellion* and of Burnet's *History of Our Own Times,* recently removed from the Sutherland Collection at the Bodleian Library to the Ashmolean Museum, Oxford.

Figures 17, 18, 21, 23 and 25 have been taken from the aquatint illustrations to *A Series of Picturesque Views of the River Thames,* 1812. Robert Havell's brother, Daniel, collaborated on these aquatints, which were made from the drawings of a third member of the family, William (1782–1857). William Havell was born in Reading, but he, like Robert and Daniel, spent his working life in London.

The anonymous mid-Victorian colour lithograph from which the illustration in Figure 19 is taken was one of a series published in celebration of the Royal Family.

Figure 26 is by William Turner (1789–1862), or 'Turner of Oxford' as he is generally known; he was born at Blackbourton, Oxfordshire, and passed almost all his active life in Oxford itself. He studied in London under Varley. He was predominantly a watercolour artist, and he is best known for the extensive series of views which he painted of Oxford and its neighbourhood.

Index

(Numerals in heavy type refer to the *figure numbers* of illustrations.)

84

33